Headlong

Headlong Theatre, in association wit
Guildford's Yvonne Arnaud Theatre present

the English game

By Richard Bean

This production was first performed at Guildford's Yvonne Arnaud Theatre on 7th May 2008

The English Game
A Comedy by Richard Bean

Sean **Tony Bell**
Bernard **Peter Bourke**
Nick **Rudi Dharmalingam**
Will **Robert East**
Alan **Andrew Frame**
Clive **John Lightbody**
Len **Trevor Martin**
Paul **Ifan Meredith**
Thiz **Sean Murray**
Olly **Marcus Onilude**
Reg **Fred Ridgeway**
Ruben **Jamie Samuel**
Theo **Howard Ward**

Writer
Richard Bean
Director
Sean Holmes
Designer
Anthony Lamble
Lighting Designer
Charles Balfour
Sound Designer
Gregory Clarke
Assistant Director
Jamie Harper
Casting Director
Gabrielle Dawes
Executive Producer
Henny Finch
Assistant Producer
Jenni Kershaw

Production Manager
Nick Ferguson
Company Stage Manager
Mike Powell-Jones
Deputy Stage Manager
Tamara Albachari
Assistant Stage Manager
Charlotte D'Arcy
Administrative Assistant
Lindsey Alvis
Costume Supervisor
Laura Hunt
Wardrobe Mistress
Beth Howard

Production LX / Re-Lighter
Chloe Kenward
Sound Technician
Nick Blount
Set Build
RK Resource Ltd
Set Transport
Paul Mathews
Lighting Hires
Stage Electrics
Sound Hires
Stage Sound Services
Production Insurance
Giles Insurance
Press
Clióna Roberts (0207 704 6224, cliona@crpr.co.uk)
Production Photography
Keith Pattison
Graphic Design
Eureka! (www.eureka.co.uk)
Image Credit
Neil McAllister / Alamy

With thanks to:
All members past and present of the Actors Anonymous Cricket Club (AACC), Fordham Sport Cricket Specialists, Aff Naseem and all at the Oval Cricket Shop, Anna Morena, *Recycling* – London's largest selection of reconditioned bicycles.

Biographies

CAST

Tony Bell
Sean

Theatre: includes *The Conservatory* (Old Red Lion); *Don Quixote* (West Yorkshire Playhouse); *Twelfth Night, The Taming of the Shrew* (Propeller/Old Vic/ BAM); *The Bee* (Soho/Tokyo Hideki Noda); *Breakfast with Johnny Wilkinson* (Chocolate Factory); *A Man for All Seasons* (Haymarket Theatre); *Red Demon* (Tokyo Hideki Noda); *A Midsummer Night's Dream* (Comedy Theatre/ BAM); *Rose Rage* (Haymarket Theatre); *Henry V, Comedy of Errors, A Winter's Tale* (Propeller); *Ghost Ward* (Almeida); *Bouncers* (Hull Truck); *Ragged Trousered Philanthropists, The Promised Land* (Sheffield Crucible); *Angels Among the Trees, Derek, Celebration* (Nottingham Playhouse); *Macbeth* (Acter Tour); *Perfect Days* (Basingstoke); *Up 'n' Under, Travels With My Aunt* (Watermill Newbury); *A Dolls House* (Harrogate Theatre); *The Mysteries* (Bolton Octagon).

Television: includes *Midsomer Murders, Holby City, Trail of Guilt, Trial and Retribution, The Bill, Peak Practice, Coronation Street, Doctors.*

Radio: includes *Stories from Italy, Love Among the Haystacks, Into Exile, White Peacock, Death of a Teenager.*

Peter Bourke
Bernard

Training: Rada

Theatre: includes *Henry IV Parts 1 and 2, Henry V, Perkin Warbeck* (RSC); *The Browning Version, Harlequinade, The Elephant Man, The Provoked Wife, On the Razzle, The Oresteia* (National); *When We Are Married, Exclusive, Dial M for Murder, Endgame* (West End); *The Merry Wives of Windsor, Racing Demon, The Sea, A Christmas Carol* (Chichester). *Bedroom Farce, Donkeys Years, One Flew Over the Cuckoo's Nest, Peace In Our Time* (Tour); *Single Spies, Volpone, Elsie and Norm's Macbeth* (Salisbury Playhouse); *Women in Mind, Picture of Dorian Gray, Gingerbread Lady* (Palace Theatre Watford); *The Inland Sea* (OSC).

Television: includes *Nicholas Nickleby, David Copperfield, The Mayor of Casterbridge, Traffic, Studio* (Anthony Minghella), *Hazel, The Bill, Dr Who.* TV Plays include *Reluctant Chickens, Incitation, America America.*

Film: includes *Stand Up Virgin Soldiers, The Stud, The Mission, SOS Titanic, Jazz Detective.*

For Fair Play Theatre Company, Peter has actor managed the West End premiere of *Endgame* and the world premieres of *Sketches by Boz* (BAC) *The Suitcase Kid* (Tricycle/Brix) and *Our State Tomorrow* (Pleasance, Edinburgh).

Rudi Dharmalingam
Nick

Theatre: includes *Rafta, Rafta* (National/Tour); *The History Boys* (National/Broadway); *Playing with Fire* (National); The title role in *Tom's Midnight Garden* (Unicorn Theatre); *The GERI Project* (Oldham Coliseum); *Learning Styles* (Impact Theatre Company); *'E To The Power 3'* (Robert Powell Theatre); *Anorak of Fire* (Adelphi Street Theatre); *The Dispute, The Tempest* (Salford University). A former member of the National Youth Theatre of Great Britain.

Television: includes *The Bill, Britz, Cutting It.*

Robert East
Will

London theatre: includes *Kean* (Apollo); *Journey's End* (Ambassadors); *Stuff Happens* (National); *The Tempest, King Lear* (Old Vic); *Richard III* (Savoy); *Twelve Angry Men* (Comedy); *An Ideal Husband* (Old Vic); *The Hothouse* (Comedy/Ambassadors); *Half The Picture, Fashion* (Tricycle); *The Sisters Rosensweig* (Old Vic); *Brand* (Aldwych); *Run For Your Wife* (Criterion); *The Common Pursuit* (Lyric, Hammersmith); *Are You Lonesome Tonight* (Phoenix); *Rosencrantz And Guildenstern Are Dead, The Real Inspector Hound* (Young Vic).

National tours: includes *Restoration* (Headlong); *The Constant Wife, Funny About Love, The Colour Of Justice, Travels With My Aunt, An Ideal Husband, Bedroom Farce*. Repertory theatre includes *Amadeus, The Clean House, Lear, The Tempest, Richard III, The Birthday Party, Don Juan* (all at Crucible, Sheffield); *Heartbreak House* (Chichester); *Hamlet* (Northcott, Exeter); *Broken Glass, Equus* (Northampton); *Our Day Out* (Playhouse, Liverpool); *Passion Play* (Wolsey, Ipswich).

Television: includes *Holby City, Charles II, The Pardoner's Tale, The Black Adder, Heartbeat, Miss Marple, Yes Minister, 'Allo 'Allo, Dave Allen At Large, Emma, Across The Lake, Oneupmanship, Rumpole, The Hothouse, Unexplained Laughter.*

Film: *Lost Illusions, Brothers and Sisters, Figures in a Landscape.*

Radio: includes *Straight Down The Middle, A Slice Of Life, A Far Cry From Brazil, Dear Penny*, all of which he also wrote, and *Going Wrong,* which he adapted.

Andrew Frame
Alan

Theatre: includes *Rough Crossings* (Headlong); *Blue on Blue* (Haymarket Basingstoke); *Market Boy, Royal Hunt of the Sun* (National); *Dead Funny* (West Yorkshire Playhouse); *Othello Landscape* (Seinendan, Tokyo); *Festen* (Lyric West End), *The Crucible* (Sheffield Crucible); *All My Sons* (York Theatre Royal); *While I Was Waiting* (BAC); *Marnie* (Haymarket Basingstoke/ Gateway Chester); *Romeo and Juliet* (Leicester Haymarket); *Small Craft Warnings* (Pleasance Theatre); *Strike Gently Away From Body* (Young Vic); *Twelfth Night* (Lyric

Belfast).

Television: includes *Trial & Retribution, The Bill, Doctors, Holby City, EastEnders, Trail of Guilt, Murder Prevention, Wire in the Blood, Dream Team, The Ideal Crush, Touching Evil.*

Radio: includes *Is He Still Breathing?, Festen, Life Together.*

John Lightbody

Clive

Trained: Drama Studio London.

Theatre: includes *Richard III* (Southwark Playhouse); *Jane Eyre* (Shared Experience); *Twelfth Night, A Doll's House, Huddersfield* (West Yorkshire Playhouse); *Taming of the Shrew, Measure for Measure, Richard III* (RSC); *Beautiful People* (Stephen Joseph Theatre); *A Christmas Carol* (Chichester Festival Theatre); *The Sea* (Minerva Theatre Chichester); *As You Like It* (National Theatre Tour); *Romeo and Juliet* (Stray Theatre); *A Little Princess* (Yvonne Arnaud/Number 1 Tour); *My Fat Friend* (Bill Kenwright Ltd); *The Admirable Crichton* (Sheffield Crucible/Chichester); *Mansfield Park* (Chichester Festival Theatre tour); *As You Like It, Incarcerator* (BAC); *She Stoops to Conquer* (Northern Stage).

Television: includes *Dalziel & Pascoe, Midsomer Murders, The Royal, Doctors, The Bill.*

Film: includes *A Bunch of Amateurs, How to lose Friends and Alienate People, The Stickup, Maybe Baby.*

Radio: includes *Things To Do Before You Die, M, Paths of Glory, Standing Sideways, Conquest of the South Pole, Clomp, I Knew Camus* (Radio 4).

Trevor Martin

Len

Theatre: includes *The Tragedy of Nan* (Orange Tree); *The Cherry Orchard* (OSC); *Anthony and Cleopatra* (Soothsayer/Clown); *Much Ado about Nothing; Jubilee, King John, Macbeth* (RSC); *Macbeth* (RSC Tokyo/USA/Young Vic); *A Midsummer Night's Dream* (RSC/World Tour); *Goldhawk Road* (Bush Theatre); *Conversations With My Father* (Stephen Joseph Theatre/Scarborough/Old Vic); *Travesties* (Savoy Theatre); *Travesties* (RSC at the Barbican); *Tamburlaine, The Taming of the Shrew, The Odyssey, Much Ado About Nothing, The Seagull* (RSC/Stratford/Barbican); *Orphans* (RSC Stratford Fringe Barbican/Waterman's Arts Centre). Earlier RSC productions include: *Cymbeline, Temptation, The Taming of the Shrew, Indigo, The Crucible, Merry Wives of Windsor, New Inn, The Winter's Tale*. Other theatre includes: *The Royal Hunt of the Sun* (Compass Theatre Company); *Long Day's Journey into Night* (Westminster Theatre); *Educating Rita, The Dresser, Duet for One* (Bristol Old Vic); *The Royal Hunt of the Sun* (Prospect Theatre Company); *King Lear, Dr Who* (Adelphi Theatre). Trevor was also a former member of the BBC Drama Repertory Company and a founder member of The National Theatre Company.

Television: includes *Doctors Christmas Special, The Romantics,*

The Bill, Swindles and Slim, Beast, Gentleman's Relish, Macbeth, Bad Blood, A Wine and a Prayer, The Ambassador, A Certain Justice, Tess of the D'Urbervilles, Dangerfield, Taggart, A Strike out of Time, Inspector Morse.
Radio: includes *The Caesars, Memento Mori, Dionysus, Dr Who – Paradise of Death, Monsieur Pamplemouse.*
Film: includes *Babel*.

Ifan Meredith
Paul

Theatre: includes *Frankenstein* (Northampton Theatre Royal); *Living Quarters* (Edinburgh Lyceum); *Mrs Pat* (Theatre Royal York); *Much Ado About Nothing* (Theatre Royal Bath); *And Then They Came For Me* (Walk Our Talk); *Journey's End* (West End); *Romeo and Juliet* (Hornchurch Queens); *The Tempest* (Almeida); *Mrs Warren's Profession* (Royal Exchange); *A View From The Bridge* (Sheffield Crucible); *Candida* (Bolton Octagon); *Loot* (Theatre of Comedy).

Television: includes *Victoria Cross Heroes, Holby City, Murder City, The Royal, Dr Jekyll & Mr Hyde, Where The Heart Is, Sirens, Peak Practice, Warriors, Great Expectations, Shadow Falls-A Mind To Kill, A Light in the Valley, The Grand, Gold, The Mill on the Floss.*

Film: includes *White on White, Metroland.*

Sean Murray
Thiz

Trained: Guildford School of Acting
Theatre: includes *The Home Place* (Comedy Theatre); *Buried Child* (National); *Jane Eyre* (Shared Experience Tour); *The Crucible* (Centreline Tour); *The Cherry Orchard* (Albery Theatre/Tour); *The Cherry Orchard, The Phoenician Woman, The Virtuoso, Two Gentlemen of Verona, Romeo & Juliet, A Woman Killed With Kindness, Amphibians* (Barbican); *The Terrible Voice of Satan* (Royal Court); *Othello, The Comedy of Errors, The Life of Galileo, The Rivals, Tartuffe, Judy, Androcles and The Lion, A Little Hotel On The Side, Maxime, School for Scandal* (Bristol Old Vic); *The Fairy Queen* (Aix-en-Provence Festival); *Judy* (Greenwich Theatre); *For King & Country, The Misanthrope* (Cambridge Theatre Company).

Television: includes *Robin Hood, Casualty, Judge John Deed, Dunkirk, Holby City, Serious and Organised, The Bill, Without Motive, Silent Witness, A Wing And A Prayer, A Rather English Marriage, Berkeley Square, Peak Practice, Seaforth, Smokescreen, Advocates, South of the Border, The Country Boy.*

Film: includes *The Truth, Finding Mallory, Hamlet.*

Radio: includes *Starlight's Apprentice, Imagine, The Chimes.*

Marcus Onilude
Olly

Trained: Laine Theatre Arts.

Theatre: includes *Safe* (West Yorkshire Playhouse); *Script Slam* (Soho); *Gone Too Far* (Royal Court). Whilst training, theatre includes *Jesus Hopped the A Train, A View from the Bridge* (Arcola).

Film: includes *Done Good, Asylum Project.*

Fred Ridgeway
Reg

Theatre: includes *Henry V, Port* (Royal Exchange); *Coriolanus* (RSC); *The Glass Room* (Hampstead Theatre); *In Extremis, Anthony & Cleopatra* (Globe); *Speaking Like Magpies, Believe What You Will, A New Way To Please You, Thomas More* (RSC/West End); *The Solid Gold Cadillac* (Garrick Theatre); *My Boy Jack* (UK Tour); *Singer* (OSC); *Christmas* (Bush); *Arms and the Man* (Touring Partnership); *Absolutely! Perhaps* (Wyndham's); *Outside Edge* (New Vic Theatre); *The Star Throwers* (Stephen Joseph Theatre); *The Weir, Spinning Into Butter* (Royal Court); *The Price* (Bolton Octogan); *Troilus and Cressida* (Tour & Old Vic); *The Rise and Fall of Little Voice* (Everyman Theatre Liverpool); *The Imposter* (Plymouth Theatre Royal); *Loot* (Chichester/West End); *Saturday, Sunday, Monday* (Chichester); *Dealer's Choice* (WYP); *My Boy Jack* (Hampstead); *Swamp City* (Birmingham Rep); *The Alchemist* (Birmingham Rep/National).

Television: includes *My Boy Jack, The Verdict, Trial and Retribution, Casualty, Spooks II, The Royal, EastEnders, Inspector Lynley Mysteries, The Bill, Peak Practice, Never Never, Midsomer Murders, Small Potatoes, Heartbeat, Father Ted.*

Film: includes *The Kinky Boot Factory, Monk Dawson, A Twist in the Tail.*

Jamie Samuel
Ruben

Training: Arts Educational School of Acting.

Theatre: includes *The Conservatory* (Old Red Lion). Whilst training, theatre includes *Gormenghast, Nana, A Midsummer Night's Dream, Jekyll & Hyde, Romeo and Juliet, The Lover, Lady Windermere's Fan, Once In A Lifetime, Metamorphosis, Three Sisters, Someone Who'll Watch Over Me.*

Films: *The Coward, Truth in the Rumour, Till the End.*

Howard Ward
Theo

Theatre: includes *Little Shop of Horrors* (Manchester Library); *Death of a Salesman* (Nottingham Playhouse); *Chicago* (Leicester Haymarket); *Pale Horse, Attempts on her Life, Faith, Night Owls, A Day in Dull Armour, Incomplete and Random Acts of Kindness* (Royal Court); *Speculators, The Great White Hope, The Triumph of the Egg, The Balcony,*

The Fair Maid of the West, The Two Noble Kinsmen, As You Like It, All's Well that End's Well (RSC); *Night of the Iguana, Macbeth, Mountain Giants, Wind in the Willows, Johnny on the Spot, The Mysteries, The Good Hope, War Horse* (National); *Neville's Island* (Watford Palace); *Six Degrees of Separation* (Manchester Royal Exchange); *Spring Awakening* (Young Vic); *The Prayer Room* (Birmingham Rep/Edinburgh Lyceum); *Coriolanus, Under the Black Flag* (Globe); *Fabulation, How Long is Never?* (Tricycle Theatre); *Heartbreak House* (Watford Palace); *A Couple Of Poor, Polish Speaking Romanians* (Soho). Howard has also directed *The Sociable Plover* and *The Fabulist* (Old Red Lion Theatre).

Television & Film: includes *Minder, London's Burning, Between The Lines, EastEnders, Insiders, Holby City, Absolute Power, Casualty, Doctors, Peak Practice, Jakes Progress, This is Personal, The Bill, Murder Investigation Team, Burnside, A Great Deliverance- The Inspector Lynley Mysteries, Unconditional Love, Amnesia, Family Affairs, The Government Inspector, Heartbeat, Ghost Squad, Cashback, The Broken.*

Radio: includes *Beware of the Trains, The Archers, Let's Move.* Directed *The Taxman* (Sony Award Nominee), *The Last Dare.*

CREATIVE TEAM

Richard Bean

Writer

Richard was born in Hull in 1956 and has worked in a variety of professions including Occupational Psychology, stand-up-comedy, and Playwriting. He is a founder member of the Monsterists – a campaigning group of playwrights lobbying for more and bigger opportunities for living playwrights. His most recent work includes *In the Club* (Hampstead); *Up on Roof* (Hull *Truck*, nominated TMA award- Best Play); *Harvest* (Royal Court winner of Critics' Circle award – Best Play); *Honeymoon Suite* (Royal Court/English Touring Theatre, winner of the Pearson Play of the Year Award); *The God Botherers* (Bush); *Smack Family Robinson* (Newcastle Live); *Under the Whaleback* (Royal Court, winner of the George Devine award 2002); *Le Pub, The Mentalists* (Lyttleton Loft, National); *Mr. England* (Sheffield Crucible); *Toast* (Royal Court); *Of Rats and Men* (Canal Café Theatre, Edinburgh Fringe); *Paradise of Fools* (Unicorn Arts Theatre).

Radio: *Yesterday* (2006); *Unsinkable* (BBC Radio 3 Wire); *Robin Hood's Revenge* (Radio 4); *Of Rats and Men* (Radio 4 Monday Night Play); *Control Group Six* (Comedy Sketch Show, 2 series).

Richard has played cricket for Hull Grammar School 2nd XI; STC/New Calypsonians (Morrant Middlesex League) and Actors Anonymous (Sunday Friendly circuit). He retired three years ago having no functional cartillage remaining in his left knee.

Sean Holmes
Director

Theatre: includes *The Man Who Had All The Luck* (Donmar Warehouse); *The Entertainer* (Old Vic); *The Caucasian Chalk Circle, Translations, The Mentalists* (National); *Julius Caesar, A New Way To Please You, Richard III, Measure for Measure, The Roman Actor* (RSC); *Incomplete and Random Acts of Kindness* (Royal Court); *Moonlight and Magnolias, The Price* (Tricycle); *The Contractor, Comedians, Sergeant Musgrave's Dance, Singer, Cleansed, Home* (OSC); *A Christmas Carol, In Celebration, The Sea, Aristocrats* (Chichester).

Anthony Lamble
Designer

Theatre credits include: *The Common Pursuit* (Menier Chocolate Factory); *Playboy of the Western World* (Abbey/ Dublin); *The Entertainer* (Old Vic); *Someone Who'll Watch Over Me* (West End); *The Price* (West End/Tricycle/tour); *Caucasian Chalk Circle, Translations* (& tour), *Sing Yer Heart Out For the Lads, A Midsummer Night's Dream, As You Like It* (National); *Measure for Measure, Richard III, The Roman Actor* (& Gielgud), *King Baby* (RSC); *The World's Biggest Diamond, Incomplete and Random Acts of Kindness, Mother Teresa Is Dead, Herons* (Royal Court); *Romeo and Juliet* (Globe/UK/European tour); *Everything is Illuminated* (Hampstead); *All Mouth, Breakfast with Jonny Wilkinson* (Chocolate Factory/Edinburgh Festival); *Cleansed, Home, Serjeant Musgrave's Dance, Singer* (& Tricycle) *Comedians, The Contractor, Troilus and Cressida* (OSC); *A Christmas Carol, In Celebration, Aristocrats, Spell of Cold Weather, The Sea, School of Night, Insignificance, The King of Prussia, Retreat from Moscow* (Chichester); *Lettice and Lovage, Exquisite Sister, Burning Everest* (WYP); *Macbeth* (Dundee); *Card Boys, All of You Mine, Mortal Ash, Pond Life, Not Fade Away* (Bush Theatre); *Biloxi Blues, Heartbreak House, Hamlet, Whole Lotta' Shakin'* (Belgrade Coventry). Dance and Opera includes: *Facing Viv* (English National Ballet); *L'Orfeo* (Japan tour); *Palace in the Sky* (ENO); *Broken Fiction* (Royal Opera House).

Charles Balfour
Lighting Designer

Theatre: includes *I'll Be the Devil* (RSC/Tricycle); *The Ugly One* (Royal Court); *Angels in America* (Headlong); *A Doll's House, A Christmas Carol and Son of Man* (Northern Stage); *Glee Club* (New Vic); *Flint Street Nativity, The Tempest, The Lady of Leisure* (Liverpool Playhouse); *The Duchess of Malfi, Don Quixote, Hedda Gabler* (WYP); *Cleansed* (OSC); *Hair, Woyzeck, Witness* (Gate); *Amadeu, Masterclass* (Derby Playhouse); *Baby Doll, Therese Raquin, Bash* (Citizens Theatre); *Country Music* (Royal Court); *Through the Leaves* (Southwark Playhouse/Duchess/

West End).

Dance: includes 24 works for Richard Alston Dance Company (Sadlers Wells/New York/ worldwide); *Eden/Eden* (Wayne McGregor/San Francisco Ballet/ Stuttgart Ballet); *Women in Memory and White* (Rosemary Butcher/Tate Modern Turbine Hall/Worldwide); *Sheer Bravado* (Alston/Ballet Theatre Munich); *Bloom* (Aletta Collins/Rambert); *Four Seasons* (Oliver Hindle/ Birmingham Royal Ballet).

Music: includes *Saul* (Opera North); *The Birds* (Opera Group); *Silence, Night and Dreams* (Zbigniew Preisner/Barbican); *Jordan Town* (Errollyn Wallen/Royal Opera House); *Writing to Vermeer* (London Sinfonietta/QEH) and Thimble Rigging (Scott Walker/ Meltdown).

Gregory Clarke
Sound Designer

The Vortex (Apollo), *Ring Round The Moon* (Playhouse), *Blackbird* (Tour), *Cloud Nine* (Almeida), *Pygmalion* (American Airlines, Broadway), *Equus* (Gielgud); *Journey's End* (London and Broadway, New York Drama Desk Award winner for Outstanding Sound Design); *A Voyage Round My Father* (Wyndham's); *The Philanthropist* (Donmar); *Hayfever, Lady Windermere's Fan, The Royal Family* (Theatre Royal, Haymarket); *And Then There Were None, Some Girls* (Gielgud); *Waiting For Godot* (New Ambassadors); *What the Butler Saw* (Criterion); *The Dresser* (Duke Of York's); *Amy's View, You Never Can Tell* (Garrick); *National Anthems* (Old Vic); *Betrayal* (Duchess); *Abigail's Party* (New Ambassadors); *The Changeling* (Barbican); *Pygmalion, Measure For Measure, Habeas Corpus, Private Lives, Much Ado About Nothing, Design for Living, As You Like It* (The Peter Hall Company); *Uncle Vanya* (Rose, Kingston) *No Man's Land, Tristan and Yseult, The Emperor Jones* (Royal National Theatre); *Great Expectations, Coriolanus, The Merry Wives of Windsor, Tantalus and Cymbeline* (RSC).

Headlong

HEADLONG: hedl'ong/ noun 1. with head first, 2. starting boldly, 3. to approach with speed and vigour.

Headlong Theatre is dedicated to new ways of making theatre. By exploring revolutionary writers and practitioners of the past and commissioning new work from artists from a wide variety of backgrounds we aim constantly to push the imaginative boundaries of the stage. Under the Artistic Directorship of Rupert Goold (Olivier Award winner for Best Director, 2008), Headlong makes exhilarating, provocative and spectacular new work to take around the country and around the world.

'Rupert Goold is one of the most exciting young talents in British theatre today' Times

'Wild, mad and deeply intelligent theatre' Sunday Times

'Tackling issues with extraordinary theatrical audacity... a company that clearly intends to continue boldly' Financial Times

COMING SOON FROM HEADLONG:

... ***SISTERS*** by Anton Chekhov, adapted and directed by Chris Goode. Gate Theatre: 5th June - 5th July 2008

SIX CHARACTERS IN SEARCH OF AN AUTHOR by Luigi Pirandello, adapted by Rupert Goold and Ben Power, directed by Rupert Goold. Minerva Theatre Chichester: 28th June – 23rd August 2008

EDWARD GANT'S AMAZING FEATS OF LONELINESS by Anthony Neilson, directed by Steve Marmion. On tour in autumn 2008 / spring 2009.

KING LEAR by William Shakespeare, directed by Rupert Goold. Featuring Pete Postlethwaite. Everyman Theatre Liverpool: 30th October – 29th November 2008.

Headlong Theatre is:
Artistic Director **Rupert Goold**
Executive Producer **Henny Finch**
Finance Manager **Julie Renwick**
Literary Associate **Ben Power**
Assistant Producer **Jenni Kershaw**
Administrative Assistant **Lindsey Alvis**

For more information or to join our mailing list, please go to www.headlongtheatre.co.uk.
You can also contact us on 020 7438 9940 or info@headlongtheatre.co.uk

The Yvonne Arnaud Theatre is one of the UK's leading producing theatres. Since 1991 it has created 124 productions (including 66 new plays), which have toured to 80 different cities in the United Kingdom providing 706 weeks of product for other regional theatres. Of the 124 productions, 54 then transferred to London, 33 of which were new plays. Its scenery workshops, in addition to creating sets for the Yvonne Arnaud's stage, have built for Glyndebourne, the Royal Shakespeare Company, Chichester Festival Theatre and most of the country's leading commercial companies.

Director and Chief Executive	**James Barber**
General Manager	**Brian Kirk**
Chief Finance Officer	**Sarah Gatward**
Funding Executive	**Madeleine Coleman**
Operations Manager	**Nick White**
PA to Director	**Dawn Kerry**
Assistant to General Manager	**Carmela Amaddio**
Head of Sales & Marketing	**Dan McWilliam**
Box Office Manager	**Sarah Stephens**

Guildford's Yvonne Arnaud Theatre gratefully acknowledges the generous support of Guildford Borough Council, ACE SE and the Foundation for Sport and the Arts.

www.yvonne-arnaud.co.uk

THE ENGLISH GAME

First published in 2008 by Oberon Books Ltd
521 Caledonian Road, London N7 9RH
Tel: 020 7607 3637 / Fax: 020 7607 3629
e-mail: info@oberonbooks.com
www.oberonbooks.com

A catalogue record for this book is available from the British Library.

ISBN: 978-1-84002-853-9

Cover design by Eureka!

Image credit Neil McAllister/Alamy

Printed in Great Britain by CPI Antony Rowe, Chippenham.

Characters

WILL	59
LEN	89
THIZ	55
PAUL	28
NICK	25
SEAN	40
CLIVE	35
ALAN	45
REG	59
THEO	55
OLLY	28
THIEF	15
RUBEN	13
BERNARD	55

It would be desirable to have supernumeries both to play the opposition team, and passers by, but the play can be done without them.

SET DESIGN

A London park cricket pitch. The action takes place in and around a section of the boundary where The Nightwatchmen cricket team congregate. The wicket is not visible. There is no boundary line. Upstage is a wire or metal fence, with holes in it, and beyond that a small copse. The grass of the pitch is not well cut and lines of cut grass remain on the pitch. A fresh pile of dog dirt is set centre stage.

Downstage right is the remains of a burnt-out cricket pavilion. All that can be seen of it is the concrete foundations, and some charred wooden floorboards. The actors always take the field down the pavilion steps, it is a club tradition, and so a batsman going out to bat exits stage right and is heard to click with his boot studs on the concrete steps.

SOUND DESIGN

The audience in the stalls should feel that they are on the pitch, and that the game is going on around them. A character fielding at Deep Long On who shouts or says anything should sound as if he is diametrically opposite a character fielding at Deep Third Man. (I guess the term is 'surround sound.)

TIME

The Present. The first two acts take place in real time. Leaps of time in the third act can be indicated by an accelerated scoreboard. All three acts take place on the same very hot August Sunday.

What men or Gods are these? What maidens loth?
What mad pursuit? What struggle to escape?
What pipes and timbrels? What wild ecstacy?

John Keats,
'Ode on a Grecian Urn'

Cricket civilises people and creates good gentlemen. I want everyone to play cricket in Zimbabwe; I want ours to be a nation of gentlemen.

Robert Mugabe – African politician
(In *The Sunday Times,* 26 February 1984)

Act One

The sound of traffic mixed with birdsong, then a cuckoo. A VW camper van pulls up off. The van's stereo plays 'And the Healing has Begun' by Van Morrison. This is turned off after a few bars, and WILL is heard humming/singing to himself the same song. He enters. He is a fifty-nine year old grey-haired man. He is wearing shorts, leather sandals and has elasticated bandages on both knees. He wears a beaten-up straw hat on his head, no sunglasses. He is carrying his own kit bag and a deckchair. WILL's cricket bag, a Slazenger, contrasts with his persona in the sense that it is newish, sleek, in a loud red. He puts the kitbag down upstage centre at the point where the slope begins. He looks out to the pitch and up at the clear sky. He breathes. He then walks downstage left and in setting up the deckchair shows an awareness of the position of the sun. He turns to go back to the camper van and sees the dog dirt which he marks with a seagull feather. He exits back to the camper van. He re-enters this time carrying his father, LEN. LEN is eighty-nine and very frail. He is dressed in a white linen suit with a white bowling cap. WILL puts him in the deckchair and makes sure that the sun is not in his eyes.

WILL: I brought both sunglasses. Which ones do you want?

LEN: The Roy Orbisons.

WILL reaches into his pocket and puts a pair of black Ray-bans on LEN's nose.

WILL: Have you got your water?

WILL finds the water bottle in his dad's jacket pocket.

LEN: (*Barely audible.*) Cup.

WILL exits to the camper van, walking deftly round the dog dirt. WILL returns with all the tea things: folding table, ice box, and in his mouth a polythene tube bag of paper cups. He puts the tea things down near his kitbag, extracts a cup and comes over to LEN with it.

WILL pours some water into the cup and puts it into LEN's hand.

LEN: (*Hardly audible.*) Rain's forecast.

WILL: It's not raining now. It's very very hot. Put this sun block on.

WILL starts to apply sun block to LEN's hands, ears and nose. LEN weakly pushes him away. WILL manages to dab some block on his nose. WILL turns and walks back to the camper van. Mid-walk he breaks into a warm-up jog, which doesn't go too well, so he goes back to walking. LEN, with a supreme effort, wipes the sun block off with his sleeve. WILL returns, this time carrying the scoreboard which is a plain piece of black wood. It's a bit tatty, worn and past its best. The number plates are in their own home-made box. WILL positions the scoreboard stage right. He turns to walk back to the camper van and stands in the dog dirt.

Bugger!

He slips his shoe off and walks up to the hedge and wipes it in the grass at the top of the bank. He exits to the van. LEN begins to unwrap a mint. WILL returns from the van carrying three bags of sandwiches all contained in the original bread bags, and his own chair which is a fishing-style chair. There are also boxes of Mr Kipling cakes from Tescos, enough for 22 but no more. The food he puts on the table. He then erects his own fishing chair. It looks as if he's going to sit in it and take a breather, but he changes his mind and exits back to the van.

LEN: (*Looking at the sky.*) There in't no rain in that sky.

Enter THIZ. His hair is thinning dyed blond. He wears sunglasses and hippy-style cotton trousers and leather sandals. He is carrying his cricket gear in a quality leather holdall, not a cricket bag, and he has his bat which is brand new still in its polythene cover. He sits in the fisherman's chair. And lets out a sigh.

THIZ: Alright Len?!

LEN: I said it'll never rain today.

THIZ: Don't want it to rain do we.

THIZ rolls his trousers up and takes his shirt off. He has a new tattoo of a bass guitar on his left shoulder. He looks at it. He stretches out and points his body to the sun.

Kaw! Lovely.

WILL re-enters carrying the kit bag. It is a typical team cricket bag and should be carried by two men at least. He shuffles along with it.

How d'yer get ninety-nine old biddies to say 'you bastard!' simultaneously?

WILL: Dunno. How do you get ninety-nine old biddies to say 'you bastard!' simultaneously?

THIZ: Get the hundredth to shout 'Bingo!'

WILL laughs. THIZ waits a beat and then laughs louder.

Am I sitting in your chair?

WILL: I haven't finished.

THIZ: Do you want a hand?

WILL: Nearly done.

THIZ: I don't wanna help. I'm just saying. Good chair this. I'm gonna get one of these.

WILL exits to the camper van. He re-enters carrying the boundary markers, and other equipment.

WILL: You can put the stumps out if you want.

THIZ: Na, I'd get it wrong.

WILL: How could you get it wrong?

THIZ: I'd put four stumps at one end and two at the other. Lovely day.

WILL: Rain's forecast.

During the next WILL goes to the tea table and empties food from a plastic carrier bag. He takes the carrier in his hand and collects the dog dirt, and puts it in the council bin.

THIZ: This is why I'm in England you know. Cricket. Nothing else.

WILL picks up THIZ's new bat.

WILL: New bat?

THIZ: Two hundred and forty quid. Is that a lot?

WILL tries the bat, testing the pick up, two or three times, and once with just the left hand.

WILL: Nice pick up.

THIZ: Yeah?

WILL suddenly rocks back and, like Brian Lara, hooks an imaginary ball with extraordinary violence.

WILL: Have you knocked it in?

THIZ: Have I what?

WILL goes to the kitbag and returns with the knockerinner. He picks up the bat and knocks it five or six times. Then hands the bat and knockerinner to THIZ.

WILL: Twenty-five hours they say.

THIZ knocks the bat half-heartedly several times, then stops.

THIZ: I'll pay our drummer. He likes that kind of thing.

WILL goes to the kitbag and takes out the stumps and the stump gauge and walks off stage right and down the pavilion steps. Enter ALAN. ALAN carries an ordinary sports kit bag in one hand and a large white wooden box in the other. This box is a new scoreboard which he has built. He is a man of about forty-five, fit, and wiry. He wears supermarket jeans and has a tattoo on one forearm of a lion.

ALAN: Hi.

THIZ: What's that Alan?

ALAN: I've built a new scoreboard.

THIZ: That's a shame. I was gonna build one. But you've done it now.

During the next ALAN opens out the scoreboard and sets it up. It's an ingeniously designed contraption with the box opening out to make a board and the inside of the box having the hooks for the numbers. The numbers are stored on the hooks.

Have you got enough sevens?

ALAN: Yeah.

THIZ: Seven hundred and seventy-seven for seven off twennie-seven overs, last man made seventy-seven. That's…seven sevens. If we didn't have enough sevens, it'd be a disaster. We'd all have to go home.

ALAN goes up stage and sets up the new scoreboard next to the old one. THIZ continues sunbathing with his eyes shut. Enter WILL from the pitch carrying mallet and stump gauge.

WILL: (*Doubtful.*) Terrific Alan. Don't think I've ever seen a white one.

ALAN: It's marine ply. If it rains.

WILL: Rain's forecast.

THIZ: It's got enough sevens.

ALAN sits on the grass and starts to undress, and change into his cricket gear. THIZ watches him. Enter PAUL. He is a man of about thirty dressed in drainpipe black jeans and loafer-style shoes. He is a bit Elvis, but not overly. He has newly dyed black hair. He carries a cricket 'coffin', a big black box, also new. He doesn't acknowledge anyone, or say hello. WILL, not expecting a hello, watches.

WILL: (*Mock surprised.*) Hello Paul!

PAUL: What?

WILL: Are you playing today?

PAUL: Yeah.

WILL: Nice to know.

WILL exits to the van.

PAUL: What's the matter with him?

THIZ: Time of the month. What's that?

PAUL: The vernacular term is cricket coffin. It's new. Lillywhites.

THIZ: I'm gonna get one of them. I'm gonna get one twice as big as that. How do you get ninety-nine old biddies to say 'you bastard!' simultaneously?

PAUL: How do you get ninety-nine old biddies to say 'you bastard!' simultaneously?

THIZ: Get the hundredth to shout 'Bingo!'

ALAN/PAUL/THIZ: (*Laugh.*)

PAUL: Tell the bees joke.

THIZ: Na. Lovely day.

PAUL: Actually, I'm not suited to this heat. Genetically I'm a Viking and living several hundred miles closer to the Equator than my biological optimum.

THIZ: Monotonous drizzle. That would suit you.

During the next ALAN and PAUL open their kitbags and begin to change into their whites. This is done on the grass edge with some concessions to modesty, but not a lot.

PAUL: Is that a new tattoo?

THIZ: Fender Precision bass.

PAUL: Looks like a guitar from Woollies.

THIZ: I've never liked you.

PAUL: Who are we playing?

ALAN: Farringden.

PAUL: Teachers. Took me two hours to get here. Wandsworth was gridlocked.

THIZ: Three minutes. I live just over there. How does that make you feel?

PAUL: There's pitches in Crouch End. We could play a few games in North London. Most of us live in North London.

WILL: Good idea Paul. You organise it.

THIZ: That's the end of that.

WILL: Where's Olly?

PAUL: He stayed at Barbara's last night.

THIZ: Barbara. Mmm. Nice.

Enter THIEF from stage right. He is a young man of about fifteen dressed in an ill-fitting cricket sweater, white trainers and white tracksuit bottoms with a stripe down the side. He is holding a mobile phone in his hand though he's not talking on it. He walks across the pitch five yards in front of the team, and off stage left.

I bet he's a cunt.

Enter REG from stage left. REG is a fifty-nine year old man. He is wearing terylene trousers with a crease and a white shirt with epaulets. He has tattoos on both arms, and an ostentatious ersatz Rolex. He has an intense, driven demeanor. He has his kit in a tennis bag.

REG: Reg Bowden!

WILL: We're The Nightwatchmen. Are you playing for Farringden?

REG: I'm Gary's next door neighbour. Gary Whattle? He can't play today.

WILL: So you're playing for us then?

REG: Gary said it'd be alright.

WILL: That's great Reg. Will, I'm the club skipper.

REG shakes hands. It is a crushing squeeze. He makes a point of shaking with everyone.

REG: Bit late. Sorry. Very bad RTA on the Chertsey Road.

THIZ: A what?

REG: Road Traffic Accident. Nobody gets in my way when I'm driving. Kaw!

WILL: They burnt the pavilion down. We change here now.

REG begins to change. He immediately starts stripping off standing up. It is a more ostentatious strip than the others. His kit consists of golf shoes with spikes, whites that are too big for him around the waist. He keeps on his military style white shirt.

REG: Glad to be out the house. The enemy's organised a poetry reading. Her own poems. Kaw! Any port in a storm!

THIZ: I like poetry.

PAUL: Do you bat or bowl?

REG: Bidda both. Used to play for British Telecom seconds. Won the Greater London Switch knockout cup three times on the dog – back in the old XE4A days when telephones were red and smelt of piss.

WILL: Is Gary alright?

REG: His mother's pacemaker's gone tits up. Sod's law eh?! That kind of thing never happens on a rainy Tuesday!?

Enter SEAN. SEAN is a man of about forty. Athletic but carrying a bit of weight. He carries a beat-up old cricket coffin decorated with airline stickers.

SEAN: Who ordered sunshine!

THIZ: Seanie!

WILL: Good afternoon Sean.

ALAN: Alright mate.

SEAN: I see the lazy bastard's cut the grass. Have we got eleven?

WILL: Ruben's playing. And Paul is twelfth man.

PAUL: Twelfth man?!

WILL: You didn't ring.

PAUL: Took me two hours to get here.

SEAN: You can umpire. You're doing an umpiring course.

WILL: Gary can't play. Sean this is Reg.

REG: Hi matey!

REG shakes hands. It is another big squeeze. SEAN glances at THIZ questioningly.

PAUL: Two hours. I mean Wandsworth was absolutely chocca.

SEAN: Alright Len!

LEN: Keeps low this wicket. Always has.

SEAN: You got that big hundred against the Combined Forces here didn't you Len?

LEN: Hundred and forty three.

SEAN: Not out.

LEN: And no chances.

SEAN: Still lost though didn't you! Ha!

SEAN rejoins the huddle.

REG: (*To THIZ.*) I know you don't I. Don't tell me! Rock Logic!

THIZ: Yeah.

REG: Hammersmith Palais nineteen...bloody hell, nineteen –

PAUL: – nineteen fourteen.

REG: Seventy-one? Seventy-two?

THIZ: Don't ask me. I can't remember a thing.

REG: Bugger me! One of Rock Logic! I've got the album with the seal on the front.

THIZ: Walrus.

REG: Is that a walrus?

THIZ: The album's called 'Plain Walrus'. It's not called 'Plain Seal' is it. That'd be crap.

PAUL: Why's it called 'Plain Walrus'?

THIZ: Drugs.

REG: They'll be playing 'Sunny Sunday' today!

THIZ: They'd better be. That song's my pension plan.

PAUL: Actually, I've always thought your 'Sunny Sunday' was a bit similar to 'Monday, Monday' by ...er... –

WILL: – the Mamas and the Papas.

PAUL: (*Singing.*) 'Monday, Monday, dada, dadada' and... 'Sunny Sunday, ah ha, da di da.'.

THIZ: One's about a Sunday and one's about a fucking Monday. Two completely different days of the week.

REG: Stone me! Rock Logic. What's the singer doing now?

THIZ: (*Standing, to WILL.*) Have I got time for a poo?

THIZ exits stage left.

WILL: We don't mention the singer.

REG: Goddit! Sorry.

SEAN goes for a piss. This involves him pissing through a gap in the fence into the copse. Enter NICK and OLLY from stage right. NICK is an energetic twenty five year old British-born Indian. He carries a Gunn and Moore cricket bag with a bat in the sleeve. He is wearing fatigue shorts and hippy sandals, and various rave accessories. OLLY is about thirty, black British, and wearing summer casuals. OLLY is hung over and crashes out next to his kit.

WILL: Niranjan! Welcome back!

SEAN: (*From the copse, mid-piss.*) Hello Nick!

NICK: Hi team!

ALAN: Alright mate.

PAUL: You've been badly missed. We've lost the last three games.

WILL: Yes, we've struggled without the Hindu God of flawlessness.

NICK: Don't worry. Fifty today. My first ever fifty. I've had coaching. Lords.

WILL: Coaching?!

NICK: New scoreboard Alan. Fantastic! Look at it. It's a work of beauty. Art.

WILL: You're not talking Olly?

OLLY: No.

WILL: Heavy night?

OLLY: Don't shout man.

WILL: You're not opening the bowling then?

OLLY: No. Leave me alone.

PAUL: (*To OLLY.*) You left the iron on in your room. It's been on two days. I could've died.

OLLY: Did you turn it off?

PAUL: I'm going to have to get a new lodger, because you're getting married.

OLLY: Yeah, you are yeah.

REG heads to the lip of the stage and stares out at the pitch. He essays a huge forward defensive shot bringing the bat down like the white cliffs of Dover.

REG: Field of bloody dreams eh?

WILL shows REG the pavilion.

WILL: Reg. We have two club rules. Rule one is that we always take the field, and leave the field, by the pavilion steps. Tradition. Burning down public facilities for a laugh whilst out of your head on skunk is integral to yoof culture, and of course, I respect that, but if we allow them to change the way we live, then we have handed them victory.

REG: If I had my way, I'd lock 'em up, and throw away the door. What's rule two?

WILL: No woman is allowed to make the tea. We're a team of militant feminists. Niranjan, this is Reg, Gary's next door neighbour.

REG: Niranjan?

NICK: Nick.

REG: Alright mate? Are you an Hindu?

NICK: My parents are Hindu.

REG: I was in Bangalore only last year. Kaw! They're all mad aren't they!

SEAN and NICK hug. REG gives NICK his huge handshake, possibly firmer because he's Indian. NICK pulls a face afterwards.

NICK: Hiya big fellah!

SEAN: Hi Nick. Hi Olly?! Is he alright?

NICK: Tequila –

SEAN: – Great.

NICK: Don't interrupt. And cocaine.

SEAN: Fuck.

Enter CLIVE. CLIVE is a well-dressed man of about thirty-five. He carries a Newbury cricket bag with bat in the sleeve, a copy of the Sunday Independent and a hard back book. PAUL is reading a paperback.

CLIVE: Hello boys. No need to stand.

SEAN and CLIVE hug. REG watches even more puzzled.

SEAN: Good to see you.

ALAN: Alright mate.

WILL: Clive!

NICK: Alright man!

CLIVE: Iceland?

NICK: Spectacular man! Got back Monday. In the nets at Lords Tuesday morning.

CLIVE: Coaching?

NICK: Yup. Fifty today, man.

PAUL: (*To CLIVE.*) Did you come through Wandsworth?

CLIVE: Yes, Paul, I did.

PAUL: I was stuck there for nearly an hour.

CLIVE: I find it somewhat churlish to complain about the traffic when one is a constituent part of same. But yes, concur, Wandsworth was a bitch!

PAUL: Rain's forecast.

CLIVE: We'd better all go home then. I didn't know you could read Paul.

PAUL: Steve Waugh's autobiography. Have you read it?

CLIVE: I wouldn't pay to watch James Joyce bat so I don't see why I should concern myself with Steve Waugh's prose.

PAUL: A psychologist helps him prepare mentally before he goes out to bat.

CLIVE: He should try having a shit and washing his hands, works for me!

PAUL: It's important to feel OK about yourself.

CLIVE: Feeling 'OK' about myself is not a state to which I aspire. Feeling fucking brilliant about myself might be worth the effort, but since that's how I feel anyway, I don't see the point.

PAUL: What are you reading?

CLIVE: I'm re-reading *The Odyssey*. Homer.

PAUL: Is that work?

CLIVE: Pleasure.

PAUL: Are you reading it in the original Latin?

CLIVE: So far he's sticking to the Greek.

WILL: Working Clive?

CLIVE: 'Yes', I'm working, 'No', I'm not being paid.

NICK: I saw it Thursday. It's really good man.

CLIVE: I didn't know you were in.

NICK: Cameron was tired. We decided to get an early night.

REG flinches.

CLIVE: I'm not overly offended.

OLLY: What is it?

CLIVE: It's a staggeringly bad translation of an incredibly poor French play. I play 'Man' and 'Dog'. An impossibly gorgeous and astonishingly intelligent actress called Katrina plays 'Woman' and 'Sparrow'.

SEAN: Does the dog shag the sparrow?

CLIVE: Not yet.

SEAN drops his pants and bends over his cricket coffin. CLIVE is left staring at his bare arse.

That's what I like about you. Your arse!

SEAN: Public school!

Enter RUBEN on his bike. He is a thirteen year old boy, already dressed in his cricket gear.

CLIVE: Ruben!

ALAN: Hello mate.

SEAN: Hiya kid!

RUBEN: Hi.

RUBEN goes over to WILL.

Dad. Where's my bat?

WILL: In the van. Say hello to your grandad.

RUBEN walks off to find his kit. Having found his kit he plays with the new scoreboard.

SEAN: Here they are! Late.

Everyone looks towards stage right to see Farringden arriving.

WILL: (*Holding up a carrier bag.*) Valuables bag. I'll lock it in the van.

No-one takes any notice. He puts his own watch and wallet in it.

Are you getting changed Paul?

PAUL: You said I was twelfth man.

WILL: I was punishing you. It's a club rule and it's good manners. You ring by Thursday to confirm that you're playing. Get changed.

SEAN: (*To WILL.*) We don't want to field first in this heat.

WILL: What's his name, their captain? History teacher. Very pedantic. Good at spelling.

CLIVE: Bernard.

WILL: Always *forgets* to bring a new ball. Possibly because they cost fifteen pounds each.

They all now get changed if not already changed. SEAN's kit is none too clean. ALAN and REG are practicing upstage, ALAN bowling to REG's batting. CLIVE approaches LEN. PAUL watches this with interest, with a glance towards OLLY.

CLIVE: What a beautiful day Len?

CLIVE shakes his hand.

LEN: Clive. Alright son.

CLIVE: Lovely. England.

LEN: Aye.

PAUL approaches.

PAUL: (*Ignoring LEN.*) I need someone to look at my best man speech for Olly's wedding.

CLIVE: Paul. Have you said hello to Len yet, today?

PAUL: Alright Len. 'Cos you're like, a trained actor –

CLIVE: I'm not *like* a trained actor, I am a trained actor.

PAUL: Alright, whatever, I thought it'd be a good idea if you had a look at it and er…make any suggestions, yeah?

CLIVE: And you want me to do this today?

PAUL: Yeah. Ta. Don't show Olly yeah.

He hands over three pieces of A4 stapled together, and walks back to the group. CLIVE opens the pages and has a quick look before putting the speech in his pocket.

SEAN: Who are we missing?

WILL: We have a quorum. Theo's here. Late, but here. Church warden you see.

SEAN: Is he?

WILL: I think he and Deborah are doing some kind of job share. Oh hell! I don't know. What's next?! Bernard.

WILL walks off stage right to meet the opposition. Enter THEO. He is a fifty-five year old rotund man. He carries his kit in a Kookaburra cricket bag with a bat in the sleeve.

THEO: Hello boys, I'm late, sorry, mea culpa. After church went to Asda, big mistake, lost the will to live. Hello Sean. What a simply splendid day!

SEAN: Alright Theo.

Enter THIZ.

THIZ: How do you get ninety-nine old biddies to say 'yer bastard!' simultaneously?

THEO: I don't know Thiz. How do you get ninety nine old biddies to say 'yer bastard!' simultaneously?

THIZ: You get the hundredth one to shout 'Bingo!'.

Most laugh. But most of all THIZ laughs loudest.

THEO: Excellent! Are we going to get the bees joke today?

OLLY: Go on Thiz. Tell the bees joke.

THIZ: Na, not today.

PAUL: Actually, the British bee population is down seventy per cent.

NICK: Why's that man?

THIZ: Tight underpants.

THEO: Thiz my dear, I never know why you spend your summers here when you could be in that lovely house of yours in the south of France.

THIZ: She got the Lot mate.

OLLY: You own a house in France don't you Theo?

THEO: Indeed we do. In the Perigord.

OLLY: That's the Dordogne isn't it?

THEO: Yes, that's right Olly, inland from Bordeaux. It's beautiful.

THIZ: Too many bloody English for my liking.

OLLY: Do you rent it out, you know, like a holiday gite?

THEO: Normally, yes, we do, but next year, we're having the roof done. In the long term we plan to live there. Just a matter of when. Thiz, a new tattoo! What is it?

THIZ: Oh piss off.

They laugh.

SEAN: What are they like, Farringden? I forget.

PAUL: They've got that fat bloke with his own tits opens the batting.

NICK: They never give him out. Never give LBWs.

SEAN: Oh yeah, I remember this lot.

OLLY: Last year he was wearing a tag. They're scared of him.

SEAN: I thought they were teachers.

THIZ: I might get a tag. Be useful, you'd always know where you were.

SEAN: Is Will going to skipper?

CLIVE: You know perfectly well that he'll ask you to skipper.

SEAN: Don't mind. We'll try and win for a change, eh?

CLIVE: Certainly. Shall we inspect the wicket?

CLIVE and SEAN put some distance between themselves and the others.

SEAN: Don't want to field first in this bloody sun.

CLIVE: *Mon brave.* What is it? You can tell me.

SEAN: No change. I can't stand it. I just can't stand it anymore.

CLIVE: If you left, no-one would blame you.

SEAN: How do you leave?

CLIVE: Plenty of people do.

SEAN: They've been playing football on here haven't they? Bastards.

WILL: (*To SEAN and CLIVE.*) Senior Professional, Senior Amateur! Boundary markers please.

CLIVE and SEAN take boundary markers off WILL, share them out, and CLIVE sticks one in the grass in front of LEN.

CLIVE: See you in the middle.

SEAN: Yup.

CLIVE places a second boundary marker in front of the pavilion and exits stage right. SEAN exits stage left placing a marker just before the wings stage left. RUBEN approaches LEN.

RUBEN: Hi Grandad.

LEN: Are they gonna give yer a game Ruben?

RUBEN: Yeah.

LEN: Wear a cap, in this sun. The worst thing on an 'ot day like this is to drop a catch 'cos the sun's in your eyes. What do yer catch with?

RUBEN: Your eyes.

LEN: What do you bat with?

RUBEN: Your eyes.

LEN: What do you bowl with?

RUBEN: Your arse.

LEN: Good lad! Ha, ha! Freddie Trueman, big arse; Darren Gough, big arse; I do not know how that Steve Harmison even gets the ball down yon end.

RUBEN: Drink some water Grandad.

RUBEN returns to the huddle.

REG: Is that the opposition?! Looks like the bloody United Nations.

NICK: Come on guys. Catching!

THIZ goes on to the pitch with his new bat. The others bar OLLY – who remains crashed out – form a horseshoe around him. They throw the ball to him and he bats it back to them as catching practice. RUBEN joins in. If there is a spectacular catch, then there are cries of 'Test Class/Good catch' etc.

THIZ: Where've you been anyhow?

NICK: Iceland.

THIZ: Fish innit?

NICK: They do have fish, yeah.

THIZ: Fish and blondes.

NICK: Yeah, they've got a lot of gorgeous boys.

THIZ: When Heaven 17 supported us in Reykjavik, they didn't want to go home.

NICK: Thiz, give Reg a go.

THIZ: But this is my new bat.

REG takes it and tests the pick up. And then essays an enormous forward defensive shot.

REG: Beaudiful. Look at that, English willow. This is the mark of a craftsman! Not been knocked out by a bloody Chinaman has it!

THIZ starts to bat catches back to them.

PAUL: How much was it?

THIZ: Two hundred and forty quid.

NICK: Two hundred and forty quid!?

THIZ: Yeah, I got the last two they had.

They laugh. Enter WILL, SEAN and CLIVE from stage right.

WILL: (*Impersonating BERNARD, ie a pedant's whine.*) 'Can we play thirty-five overs with no limit on the bowlers because we've only got four bowlers?'

SEAN: We've only got one bowler.

WILL: 'Can we bat first because we've got two players lost in South West London?'

SEAN: So he wants us to field first in this heat? Oh yeah.

WILL: Sean, I don't think I can be nice to Bernard all day.

SEAN: I'll skipper.

CLIVE: I'll vice captain. I'll Gower to your Gooch.

SEAN: There's no way I'm letting them bat first. I'm not gonna gift them an advantage just 'cos they're a bunch of twats who can't read an A to Z. That's exactly what's wrong with this country. The more crap, desperate, and stupid you are the more you get given. Right, I'll go and do the toss. (*Beat.*) Haven't got a coin. You got a coin?

CLIVE gives him a fifty p piece. SEAN exits stage right.

WILL: Is he alright?

CLIVE: The usual.

WILL: How old are the kids now?

CLIVE: Three and five-ish.

REG offers the bat to someone else.

REG: I need a piss. What do I do?

THIZ: How old are you?

THEO: We go in the hedge. But try and avoid the walkers. We've had complaints.

THIZ: I've never had any complaints.

Over by the tea things.

WILL: 'Have you done vegetarian sandwiches?' 'Have you done any without butter?' One of them's strict vegan. Can't go within two yards of an animal product.

CLIVE: Won't be able to catch a leather ball then! And – have you done vegetarian sandwiches?

WILL: Course I have. We've been playing these pedants ten years.

CLIVE: Eleven years.

WILL: Don't you start.

CLIVE: It was my first game for this club. I drove down from Liverpool. Why Liverpool? Oh, it was that TIE show teaching school children that slavery is something that white people do to black people, instead of the unpalatable truth that it's what powerful people do to vulnerable people. Entirely mendacious bollocks! But it was my first acting job! Hurrah! But what a great match that was, Sean scored eighty-three, and Thiz had to go to hospital to get his jaw wired up.

WILL: Did we win?

CLIVE: I can't remember. Didn't care. I was just so happy I'd found a team.

CLIVE moves away, joins the group. Enter SEAN from stage right. Face set in a frown.

THEO: Here he comes! Now has he won the toss? One can never tell with Sean's face can one?

CLIVE: Same face for everything. Whether he's having his cock sucked or his teeth drilled.

THIZ: How d'you know?

CLIVE: We share the same dentist.

They all look at SEAN.

SEAN: Nick! Keeper's pads!

The odd groan.

THEO: Fielding!

PAUL: You lost the toss then?

SEAN: No, I won the toss, and decided to field in this heat. Course I lost the friggin toss.

PAUL: Alright.

THIZ: Eh Theo, I've got this lump in my left bollock, like a gristly lump.

THEO: Can you feel it?

THIZ: Do you wanna feel it?

THEO: I haven't washed my hands since Asda.

CLIVE: Thiz hasn't washed his balls since Glastonbury.

THIZ: Didn't do Glastonbury this year. He wouldn't have us back. Said we eat too much. It's like a gristly hard thing, like a pen top. Go on, have a feel.

THEO: Is there any bruising?

THIZ: I'll have a look.

THIZ sits on the ground, pulls his pants down and inspects his balls.

REG: Are you a doctor mate?

THEO: GP, yes.

REG: Kaw! I bet everyone, you know, eh, all the time, all their –

THEO: – I don't mind. It's why God put me on this earth.

REG: I'm in Telecoms. Big switches. Digital. Fibre ops. Yeah.

THEO: Excellent. I use the telephone a lot. Excuse me Reg, I haven't said hello to Len yet.

THEO goes over to LEN.

You need to cover your arms up Len. It's hot.

LEN: Who are you?

THEO: It's me, Theo. Roll these sleeves down. And drink some water.

THEO starts to roll his sleeves down for him.

LEN: If I drink any more water I'll need a piss.

THEO: Let us know and we'll carry you to the hedge.

LEN: You'd be too late. I played on this pitch you know.

THEO: You made a lot of runs against the Combined Forces, didn't you?

LEN: Hundred and forty-three. Not out. No chances. We had a pavilion in them days. I blame central heating.

THEO: For what? For everything?

LEN: If they all had fires indoors the kids wun't be interested.

THEO: Mmm. We're fielding.

THEO goes back to the group.

THIZ: They look perfect. Kinda beautiful in their own way.

THEO: Let me have a feel then.

CLIVE: I'm after Theo.

NICK: I'm next after Clive.

THEO puts his hand in THIZ's whites and feels. The others groan and giggle. REG doesn't know what to do.

THEO: Is that it?

THIZ: No, that's always been there. Ow!

THEO: That?

THIZ: Yeah.

THEO removes his hand, and gets a wet wipe from his bag.

THEO: Go and see your GP.

THIZ: But he doesn't like me.

THEO: It's *probably* an epididymal cyst.

THIZ: What's that? Cancer?

THEO: It's a small fibrous lump of cartilage which has formed, surprisingly enough, as a spontaneous cure. Let me think of an analogy.

THIZ: I've got an analogy?

THEO: If someone was holding a wedding party in your testicular sack, understand?

THIZ: – er…yeah –

THEO: – it's all going well, sunny day, funny vicar, when suddenly BANG! A meteorite crashes into the garden, killing dozens of people. What would happen?

THIZ: Dunno.

THEO: The police would erect a crime scene tent, a protective carapace of cartilage, then if the police forgot to take the tent away you would then be left with an epididymal cyst. Your body has healed itself. Understand?

THIZ: I bloody love you.

THEO: But, your GP will want to check your prostate and I'm not doing that for you.

THIZ: Where's my prostate?

THEO: Beyond your arse.

CLIVE: And put a shirt on.

WILL: And stop playing with your knob.

OLLY: And tell the bees joke.

NICK: And lose some weight.

THIZ: Alright!

REG: Bananas.

THIZ: I thought you were.

REG: I don't have lunch at all. I just have one banana.

THIZ: (*Miming holding a huge banana.*) One huuuuuge banana. Banana and chips please. And a banana pie…and two crunchies.

They all laugh.

REG: I've lost twenty-seven pounds in less than a year.

ALAN: Easy to eat, bananas. Nature's fast food innit.

THIZ: Lobster's difficult to eat. The RAC do not recommend lobster as a driving snack. A banana, you just chuck it on the dashboard, but a lobster, you've got to keep it fresh in a bucket on the passenger seat until that moment when you can't find the Polos, and you've run out of crisps –

At this point NICK grabs THIZ from behind and with his hand over his mouth wrestles him.

NICK: Enough lobster!

PAUL: I've never eaten lobster.

REG: I've eaten dog. In Korea. Beaudiful! They frighten it first. Frightened meat tastes better.

OLLY: How do they frighten it?

REG: Dunno.

THIZ: Every restaurant's got a sixteen-stone ginger tom cat in a shed, and they take the dogs out now and then for a look. Miaow!

SEAN: Clive! Can you open the bowling please?

CLIVE: For you, anything.

SEAN: Which end do you want?

CLIVE: Let me ponder a while. Uphill, or downhill? Downhill.

SEAN: Olly! First over the far end please.

OLLY: Uphill? I don't think I can do it.

SEAN: Do you think Freddie Flintoff turns up at Lords with a blood system that is eighty-seven per cent tequila?

CLIVE: Apparently!

THEO: Exactly!

THIZ: Course he does!

ALAN: Yeah.

NICK: That's what I've heard!

WILL: By all accounts, yes.

SEAN: Bloody hell. Thiz! Open the bowling please, uphill.

THIZ: But I've got an epididymal cyst.

SEAN: Do you want to bowl or not? I want everyone wearing a cap in this sun.

NICK picks up the scorebook and takes it over to LEN with a pencil. THEO follows quickly.

NICK: There you go Len! Alright.

THEO: You don't want to be bothered with the book today do you Len?

LEN: I'll do it if you want me to son.

THEO ushers NICK and the book back to the huddle.

THEO: He's had a bit of a downward journey the last two weeks.

NICK: Shit. Yeah?

THEO: Yup. He's here. That's enough and we should celebrate that.

Enter BERNARD from the other team.

WILL: Yes Bernard?

BERNARD: Just hoping to have a sneak preview of the new ball. Ha, ha!

WILL: Supplying the new ball is the visiting team's responsibility Bernard.

BERNARD: Was it agreed that we would supply the new ball?

WILL: Yes, you rang me last year to check. Christmas Eve.

BERNARD: It's the only time you can be sure that people are going to be in.

WILL: Would you like to *buy* one of ours?

WILL goes to get the box of balls.

BERNARD: Are they proper quartered balls?

WILL: Yes. (*Aside.*) Hung, drawn and quartered.

BERNARD picks one out.

BERNARD: Ooh, they're good ones aren't they?

WILL: Yes, they're 'fifteen pounds each' ones.

BERNARD: We'll settle up in the pub.

(*To them all.*) Hot. Glad we won the toss.

(*To WILL.*) Shall we have two drinks breaks Will?

SEAN: Alright! Yeah, after fifteen overs and and twenty-five.

BERNARD: Eleven and twenty-two would be more equidistant spacing for a thirty-five over game.

SEAN: Yeah, it would, but I want fifteen and twenty-five.

BERNARD: OK.

ALAN: I'll show you how the new scoreboard works.

BERNARD: Lovely.

ALAN and BERNARD head upstage and take the scoreboard off stage right.

THIZ: She's happy enough in't she. Sunny day like this; husband; three kids; another one on the way; bag over her head.

PAUL: Actually, technically, that's a niqab.

THIZ: Maybe that's where I went wrong with Pammy. 'Oi! Pammy! You're not going to the Brits dressed like that! Everyone can see your tits! I got you a nice niqab for Christmas!? Wear that! Or else!' I told her to do something once. Kaw! Never heard the end of it.

SEAN: Come on then!

NICK: Let's go boys!

REG heads for the middle directly out.

RUBEN: Reg!

REG: Yeah?

NICK: No.

WILL: Rule number one.

REG: Brain dead! Pavilion!

SEAN: (*Off.*) Square leg Alan. Thiz. Thiz! Fine leg.

THIZ: (*Off.*) Where's that then?

SEAN: (*Off.*) Over there, on the line. Reg, midwicket please.

REG: (*Off.*) Aye, aye cap'n.

SEAN: (*Off.*) Er…Will, the usual please. First slip. Theo, mid off.

THEO: (*Off.*) Batsmen in!

Clapping.

BATSMAN: (*Off.*) Save your energy. You'll be clapping me out in a minute. Ha!

CLIVE: (*Off.*) We won't clap you out.

BATSMAN: (*Off.*) Which end are you opening?

CLIVE: (*Off.*) I'm opening.

NICK: (*Off.*) No bails!

BERNARD: (*Off.*) We've got bails! You can use ours!

WILL: (*Off.*) No thank you Bernard. Theo, use our bails. There are new bails in the bag!

THEO enters from stage right.

LEN: Forgot the bails?

THEO: Yes Len, the traditional run off the pitch to find the bails.

THEO finds the bails and starts to run straight out on to the pitch.

LEN: Pavilion!

THEO: Oopsadaisy!

THEO turns and exits stage right, down the steps.

NICK: (*Off.*) Come on The Nightwatchmen!

SEAN: (*Off.*) On your toes, walking in! Thiz! Hands out your pockets! Walking in please!

OLLY: (*Off.*) Come on Clive!

UMPIRE: (*Off.*) Play!

CLIVE bowls. It goes wide to the keeper.

BERNARD: (*Off.*) Wide ball!

SEAN: (*Off.*) That's OK! Don't worry about it.

WILL: (*Off.*) Line OR length please Clive, one or the other!

Mild laughter. Enter the THIEF from stage left. He goes over to the pile of kit and personal belongings and sits. He then systematically and quite coolly goes through the trousers, jackets and finds the odd bits of cash and coins. LEN does not see him. Having taken a fair harvest he saunters off through the copse.

End of Act One.

Act Two

The same, two and a half hours later. Still very sunny. The new scoreboard has fifty-three in the runs section; nothing at all in the wickets section; the overs section says twelve. It is pointing sideways, and not out to the players. The old scoreboard which is alongside the new scoreboard and is standing up has 181 in the runs section; seven in the wickets section; and there is nothing in the overs section; the Last Man section reads 84. WILL is organising the tea, specifically filling a twenty cupper teapot. The Nightwatchmen are sitting around their bags eating tea from paper plates. RUBEN is somewhat off the huddle to stage right playing a computer game on a handheld; THEO is sitting in a deckchair and eating an orange; THIZ is smoking a cigar, with his shirt off, and eating cakes; NICK is rolling a roll-your-own ciggie and eating sandwiches; CLIVE is reading PAUL's speech, somewhat surreptitiously – ie, hiding it from the others and OLLY in particular. PAUL is eating a cake; SEAN is eating sandwiches and sitting on a cricket pad; OLLY is drinking from a large bottle of water, texting on his mobile and smoking; REG is eating a banana and standing; ALAN is sat slightly off to stage left and eating sandwiches, and applying a plaster to a cut. LEN has a plate of sandwiches on his lap, untouched. He is asleep.

PAUL: This tastes of almonds.

THEO: It's an almond slice.

THIZ: This bloke, right, he's a northerner –

VARIOUS: Hurrah!

SEAN: Ruben! Come over here! Quick!

RUBEN shuffles into the group.

THIZ: – goes back home, see his mum. Now he's done alright for himself in London. Got himself some shoes, and trousers, you know, he's done well. And he's walking down this street in his home town, and he sees this other bloke coming towards him, and he recognises him, and he wants to avoid this bloke cos he's a loser, and he's done well, our bloke, and he's a sensitive man is our man. But he's trapped and so he says 'Hello' to the loser and the loser says 'Hello' back. And the loser says 'Nice shoes. Nice trousers. What are you doing nowadays?' and our bloke says 'Oh you know, I'm in London, doing alright, bit of this bit of that, keeping me head above water. What about you, where are you living now'. And the loser says 'I'm living with me mam in the flats'.

NICK laughs.

'Oh', says our bloke 'and are you working?' he says. And the loser says 'Aye, I am that' and our bloke says 'And what are you doing, you know, for a job?' And the loser says 'I keep bees',

NICK laughs, OLLY laughs, others giggle.

And our bloke says 'Wow! How many bees have you got?' And the bloke says 'I've got seventeen thousand of the little buggers',

Some laughter.

And our bloke says 'Seventeen thousand bees. Kaw! Where do you keep them?' And the loser says 'In a biscuit tin in the kitchen.' And our bloke says 'How do they breathe?'

NICK is now helpless with laughter and stands and walks away and off stage left.

And the loser thinks for a second and then he says – 'Ah, fuck 'em.'

There is general laughter but REG doesn't laugh and neither does ALAN. RUBEN doesn't really laugh either. He stays where he is.

NICK: What do you think Rubes?

RUBEN: (*Having not got it.*) Yeah. It's a funny joke. Ha, ha!

OLLY: I love this.

NICK: Brilliant isn't it.

OLLY: Couple of weeks ago, you know the Dorothy's match, when we didn't play, I enjoyed that as well. I think if someone organised a club, not a cricket club, let's call it a 'grass field club' where what you do on a Sunday is drive for two hours across London traffic to a grass field then you dress up in white clothes and sit around for seven hours with your mates smoking, eating sandwiches and talking absolute bollocks, I'd join.

NICK: I'd join man.

THEO: Definitely!

CLIVE: Depends on the quality of the conversation.

THIZ: And the sandwiches.

ALAN: Why didn't we play the Dorothy's match?

SEAN: The Friends of Dorothy Cricket Club turned up and so did the Museum eleven. Both down to play us.

ALAN: No-one told me.

ALAN stands and goes over to the tea table.

SEAN: I can't believe our fixture secretary does not know that a game he organised two weeks ago did not happen. Has no-one had the balls to tell him he cocked up?

CLIVE: That's your job big fellah.

SEAN: Anyhow, do we want to play the Museum next year?

Silence.

We don't have to.

THEO: I'm sorry, I've missed something chaps. Why would we cancel the fixture?

SEAN: They had difficulty getting a team out each week so one of their Bengali players –

OLLY: – Bangladeshi.

SEAN: Sorry! One of their Bangladeshi players brought a load of his mates along and now the team is Fat Sid and ten Bangladeshis who speak to each other in Urdu and –

OLLY: – Bengali.

SEAN: Fuck! Bengali…and don't go to the pub!

THEO: I fail to see why that is any reason for us to cancel the fixture.

SEAN: Alright. Is that generally agreed? We keep the fixture?

ALAN: Course.

THIZ: Yeah, yeah.

CLIVE: Excellent.

OLLY: No problem.

NICK: Cool.

THEO: Yes we do.

SEAN: Fat Sid wants to play for us.

CLIVE: We don't need him. We've already got weakness in depth.

SEAN: The Dorothys were asking after you Nick.

THIZ: Yeah, they fancy you, Nick. Wooo!

SEAN: Be quite nice for you to play in an all-gay team wouldn't it?

NICK: No.

THIZ: All they talk about is cock.

NICK: All you talk about is women.

THIZ: What else is there?

At the tea table.

REG: The bees joke eh?

ALAN: I don't get it. Never have. Good catch.

REG: Ta. Just slapped in there, and stuck, like a firm little tit.

ALAN: You're next door to Gary, aren't you?

REG: Yeah.

ALAN: I'm in the next street. Laburnum. Yours is the one with the double garage yeah?

REG: That's the first double garage in Whitton Dean that is.

CLIVE: Reg eh?

THIZ: He's definitely gay.

REG: (*Beat.*) Nice scoreboard, are you a chippy?

ALAN: Plumber.

REG: I need a plumber. The enemy wants a sink up in the loft for her water colours. Be easy enough. There's a drain pipe comes down from the roof.

ALAN: It's illegal to plumb a soil waste into a rain water drain.

REG: No-one'll know. I'll pay cash.

ALAN: No.

ALAN walks over to the white scoreboard and starts dismantling it and putting it back together. REG, somewhat puzzled, rejoins the main group.

PAUL: I'd like to play more matches in North London, and maybe tour France again. We could stay at your house Thiz.

THIZ: I told you. Pammy got the Lot.

THEO: And I don't think she'd appreciate eleven blokes turning up on her doorstep.

THIZ: She wouldn't mind that. It's me she doesn't like. If you go, take plenty of money.

PAUL: Mick Jagger's got his own team in the Loire valley. Maybe we could play them on the way down. Do you know Mick Jagger?

THIZ: He doesn't like me, Mick. I don't like him much. His own cricket team. Who does he think he is?

CLIVE: He thinks he's Mick Jagger.

THIZ: So? Yeah? And?

REG: I saw that Jerry Hall couple of years ago in…oh bugger, what's it called –

CLIVE: B and Q.

REG: Na.

NICK: Wickes.

THIZ: A bikini.

REG: No, that play –

CLIVE: *The Graduate.*

REG: That's it. Took all her kit off she did. Yeah.

CLIVE: Did you see Ruben's catch Paul?

PAUL: What?

They giggle.

SEAN: You dropped two catches. The two openers. Their partnership was worth one hundred and twenty-seven.

PAUL: The sun was in my eyes.

SEAN: You didn't have a cap on.

PAUL: I don't like wearing a cap. I've got a sensitive scalp.

CLIVE: It's your hair. You're vain.

PAUL: I'm not vain.

CLIVE: You dye your hair!

PAUL: Actually, I thought this was a free country.

SEAN: What is the function of a cap on a cricket pitch? The brim keeps the sun out of your eyes so you can catch the opening batsman before he gets the chance to make seventy-three runs.

CLIVE: Whereas the function of your hair, your dyed hair –

PAUL: – my hair…it's about the ego ideal, which is er… Freudian. It's a kind of externalised objectification of my ideal self. Freud calls it the ego ideal. Everybody's got one.

CLIVE: So your ego ideal has got dyed hair?

PAUL: Oh, piss off.

SEAN: Clive's ego ideal is called Clive. Well bowled Theo.

NICK: Web of mystery.

THIZ: Did I bowl well?

SEAN: No. Neither did Olly.

THIZ: Oh, that's alright then.

OLLY: Thanks.

THIZ: Every other team we play, the West Indian bloke's always good. Why have we got the only shit West Indian?

NICK: Yeah. Why's that man?

CLIVE: Why are you very average Olly?

OLLY: I'm in love aren't I.

THEO: Marvellous. Marriage?

OLLY: Next month.

THEO: Excellent! The world must be peopled!

SEAN: You'll have to move out of Paul's flat.

THIZ: Paul won't know what to do without you. Live off toast.

PAUL: I won an award once for my cauliflower cheese. Burton Latimer Boys Brigade.

THIZ: Makes me fart.

THEO: This'll be the lovely Barbara then is it?

OLLY: Yup.

THIZ: (*To OLLY.*) Barbara eh?

OLLY: Yeah, Barbara.

THIZ: Is the sex good?

OLLY: Fantastic.

THIZ: Is it?

OLLY: Yeah.

THIZ: Yeah?

OLLY: Yeah.

THIZ: I love sex.

CLIVE: Excuse me boys. Theo is here. Our lay preacher. He may object to such a crude discussion of sex.

THEO: *Au contraire.* I take the gift of sex to be a compelling argument for the existence of my God. Through sex men discover love, and through love women discover sex.

THIZ: I went out with a Brenda once. She had a terrapin in a tank. Used to watch.

They laugh. REG goes over to the tea table. CLIVE watches him go.

CLIVE: Where did we find 'Reg'?

THEO: Gary's next door neighbour.

CLIVE: I didn't know Gary lived in a neolithic cave system.

THEO: That's a terrible thing to say Clive.

CLIVE: Concur. (*Shouted to REG.*) Sorry Reg!

REG: (*Halfway to the tea table.*) What?

CLIVE: Sorry!

REG: Alright.

At the tea table.

Good bunch of blokes.

WILL: They'll be talking about you now. Now you've come over here.

REG: Yeah?

WILL: Yup!

The group laugh at something. One of the group turns and looks at REG. He sees this.

Did I hear Thiz tell the bees joke?

REG: Yeah. Very funny. Great tea! The ladies done us proud! Say thank you to your wife from me. Smashing!

WILL: Rule number two Reg.

REG: Oh yeah, feminism, you made it yourself then, kaw! Well done mate! Look, if you're ever short give me a ring. For this I wouldn't bother asking the enemy, I'd just climb out the bog window and – (*Whistles.*)

WILL: Tea's ready. Sugar's there.

During the next WILL goes over to his dad and gets him to drink some tea. During the next REG goes through the hedge and into the copse where he throws up. THEO goes into the hedge for a pee.

SEAN: Len's had a bit of a dip then has he?

CLIVE: Yes. Sad. Lovely man. Paul do you think you'll have any progeny to look after you? A son to make sure you're taking in enough liquids on a hot day.

PAUL: Actually, I've thought about this, and I've decided that I'm gonna shoot myself when I'm seventy. Like that American bloke.

CLIVE: Hemingway.

PAUL: Yeah, him.

CLIVE: He was sixty.

PAUL: Was he? Still I think the moment you become a burden on the people around you, yeah, well, knowhatimean.

CLIVE: Did anyone bring a gun?

NICK: So what are we gonna do about the scoreboard then?

THIZ: What's wrong with the scoreboard?

CLIVE: It's sensationally brilliant in every aspect of design, but it fails in its one and only imperative function – you can't read the bloody numbers when you're in the bloody middle.

SEAN: White reflects the sun, blinds you.

PAUL: It just needs painting matt black.

CLIVE: (*To PAUL.*) So you're gonna tell Alan are you?

PAUL: I don't mind telling him.

ALAN returns to the huddle and starts fiddling with his gear. He has a cup of tea and cakes.

Alan?

ALAN: What?

PAUL: Nothing.

ALAN: What?

PAUL: Good catch.

NICK: Yeah, inspirational catch man.

SEAN: This new scoreboard you've built Alan.

ALAN: Yeah?

SEAN: It's terrific. But one problem. On a sunny day like this, because it's black on white, not white on black, you can't read the numbers. Did you see they swapped to using the old scoreboard half way through the innings?

NICK: I'll paint it man. Matt black. White numbers.

ALAN goes over to the scoreboard which he starts to dismantle. REG returns to the huddle.

CLIVE: (*To SEAN.*) Have you ever considered a career as a bereavement counsellor?

NICK: If there's a war man, I wanna be on Sean's side.

THIZ: I think I'd get killed in a war cos I'd do something really brave but really stupid just so people would like me a bit more.

THEO: You're terribly insecure Thiz. That's what all the joke telling's about.

THIZ: Just want to be loved.

THEO: Enoch Powell's only regret about the second world war was that he came back. That he didn't die for his country.

REG: Bloody clever man. Kaw! Enoch Powell. What a brain!

SEAN: Len came back.

REG: What the old guy?

SEAN: He was at Pegasus Bridge.

REG: Pegasus Bridge? What? No!? British Sixth Airborne?

SEAN: Dunno about that.

REG: If there's one thing I do know, it's my British military history.

(*To LEN.*) I take my hat off to you sir!

THIZ: You're not wearing a hat.

Enter BERNARD for more cakes.

BERNARD: (*To WILL*) Whose wife do we thank for a lovely tea?

WILL: Mr Kipling's.

A mobile phone goes off. Two or three of them search.

It's mine. Don't panic boys.

SEAN: I think we had seven LBW shouts, and three were bloody plumb.

CLIVE: Four.

BERNARD slopes off, unwanted.

SEAN: No-one bats like that. You stick your front foot across middle stump and hit across the line. Miss and you're out.

CLIVE: What are you suggesting Sean?

SEAN: I don't think their umpires ever had any intention of giving either one of those two openers out. I bet you those two are top of their averages.

CLIVE: Four matches to the end of the season.

WILL: (*On phone.*) RAF Wittering? OK we'll be finished about eight, if it doesn't rain…rain's forecast…where's the car?… they're my knees, I'll do what I like with them…Darling, don't you dare matronise me!…Goodbye!

He clicks the phone off. Enter ALAN to the huddle. He is in a sulk. He gathers his kit and puts it in his bag.

SEAN: What you doing Alan?

ALAN says nothing.

Oh bloody hell Alan?!

ALAN picks his kit up and walks over to the new scoreboard picks that up too, and walks off. REG rejoins the group.

Alan!

SEAN gets up and follows ALAN. WILL joins them.

THEO: Sean could start an argument in a ploughed field.

WILL: Where's Alan going?

CLIVE: Sean critiqued the new scoreboard by having a quiet word in his ear.

NICK: Which is why Alan's gone off for hospital treatment.

REG: My kinda cricketer, Sean. Look at the Aussies. Every last one of them's an evil bastard. This country's gone soft. Do you know what I blame? Pass the parcel.

NICK: Pass the parcel?

THIZ: Yeah! I agree. Pass the parcel. It's ruined this country.

REG: The parcel nowadays, if there's twelve kids, it's got twelve prizes in it. They wait their turn, they get a prize, no effort involved. When I was a kid, there was *one* prize, *one* magic bouncy ball! We used to tear at that parcel like starving dogs! Socialism.

NICK: (*As a retort.*) Thatcherism.

CLIVE: My go. Magnetism. Thiz?!

THIZ: Cannibalism.

(*Beat.*) I've never played pass the parcel. Is it difficult?

CLIVE: You've never played pass the parcel?

THIZ: I went to boarding school didn't I. I was too busy wanking. Quite a few of them ended up playing professional sport.

CLIVE: Professional sport is an oxymoron. Sport is an activity taken up for pleasure or exercise, preferably both. The gods understand, and on a Sunday, on their day off, they knock a ball about with their mates.

PAUL: *Gladiator.* What a movie! Totally compelling.

REG: British!

CLIVE: I thought it was execrable nonsense.

THIZ: You weren't in it then?

They laugh.

PAUL: Actually Clive, have you ever had a part in a film?

CLIVE: Yes. *Titanic.*

REG: British!

OLLY: Hollywood surely.

REG: Yeah, but it was a British ship.

CLIVE: Which sank.

REG: Yeah, obviously.

PAUL: Actually, the Titanic didn't sink, it was its sister ship that sank.

THIZ: Oh fuck, here we go.

PAUL: They'd identified several design faults in the Titanic, so before the maiden voyage they switched name plates with the Olympic, which they were building right alongside.

NICK: So man, the Titanic was really the Olympic?

PAUL: Exactly.

OLLY: What happened to the Olympic then?

PAUL: On it's maiden voyage, it hit an iceberg and sank.

NICK: OK man, so…what happened to the Titanic?

PAUL: It was in service for twenty-four years, then decommissioned and all the fittings sold off at auction.

THIZ: (*To PAUL.*) I'd do almost anything to get away from you.

They laugh. THEO joins WILL at the tea table.

THEO: (*To WILL.*) So what's Harriet doing today?

WILL: RAF Wittering. She's handcuffed herself to the fence.

THEO: They've got a lovely day for it.

WILL: Yeah, they all be singing now.

THEO: Will she get arrested?

WILL: Let's hope eh.

SEAN enters with their book. He is studying it.

PAUL: Lockerbie's another one.

CLIVE: – oh no!

PAUL: The bomb on flight 702 was put there by the American Drugs Enforcement Agency.

REG: I can believe that. The Yanks, eh, they don't fuck about like we do.

PAUL: The theory is contained in a book called *The Octopus Conspiracy* written by a CIA agent.

OLLY: So who put the suitcase on the plane?

THIZ: An octopus.

Some laugh.

He had eight suitcases. Got an upgrade to business class, said he didn't have enough leg room.

All laugh, including THIZ.

PAUL: It's important to retain a grip on the empirical truth in these difficult times when we are technically at war against an abstract noun, 'terrorism' and er…yeah.

CLIVE: You wouldn't recognise the empirical truth if it jumped into bed with you and fucked you up the arse.

NICK: Boys!

SEAN: What did I tell you? Pilger and Begum are neck and neck for the averages. Forty-two point three versus thirty-eight point nine. They've got three matches left. Their umpires were never going to give them out.

THIZ: Which one's Pilger?

NICK: Pilger's the one who's not Begum.

SEAN: We're being shafted here.

CLIVE: Oh darling! Please! It's a friendly.

SEAN: (*Not intense.*) You've got to play the game properly. As soon as you start tolerating bollocks, that's it. You might as well pack up and go home. (*With a mouthful of egg mayo.*) That is what it is to be moral, to be human. Surely? Brilliant egg mayonnaise Will.

WILL: Thank you.

REG: You godda a house in the south of France then Thiz?

THIZ: No. I said. She got the Lot.

THEO: (*To REG.*) Thiz is divorced. As part of the settlement his wife, Pammy, was given the house in France in the *departement* known as 'the Lot and Garonne', which Thiz, abbreviates to 'the Lot', as in 'she got the lot', which suggests that Pammy fleeced him which is untrue, and ignores the fact that she gave him three beautiful children, whilst he was bedding teenage girls from Helsinki to Hartlepool.

THIZ: Where's Hartlepool?

REG: We go to France every year. Caravan. What a beautiful country. Kaw! It's wasted on those bastards!

WILL: So, what's it like living next door to Gary, Reg?

REG: Bidda of a nutter eh?!

THEO: A saint, would be my assessment, given all that he's had to cope with.

REG: Yeah, he's got his hands full with her.

THEO: I meant Jack, the autistic child.

REG: Oh yeah! That little bugger! I've had to get a new fence. The ship lap wasn't up to it. Another cup of tea I think.

REG goes over to the tea table. THIZ is inspecting his sandwich.

THIZ: Eh Will, is this butter?

WILL: No. It's 'I can't believe it's not butter'.

THIZ: Fuck me, it's marge!?

CLIVE: Now that would be a good brand name. 'Fuck me, it's marge!' Excuse me miss, do you work here, in which aisle would I find the 'Fuck me it's Marge'?'

Some giggle.

WILL: If you had ever 'made' a cricket tea Thiz, as opposed to subcontracting the task to Harrods, you'd know that butter is difficult to spread.

THIZ: It's not my fault I'm bloody loaded.

At the tea table. THEO is clearing away and REG comes up. He is eating a banana.

REG: Well bowled matey.

THEO: Thank you Reg.

REG: You know, as a doctor, well, I've got four kids, teenagers. How can you tell if they're on drugs?

THEO: Social withdrawal, confusion, memory loss, staying in bed all day.

REG: Bloody hell, the wife's on 'em an'all!

THEO: The best way is to talk to them.

Silence, as REG considers the horror of talking to his kids.

We looked at the houses in your street.

REG: It's good for the schools, you don't get any, you know… they're all down the road. It's a good Catholic school, you know what I mean. You have to get 'em all Christened like, but you know, I'm not a racialist, but at the end of the day 'Is the Pope a Paki?' Knowhatimean?

THEO: Yours must be the one with the double garage?

REG: Yeah, that's the first double garage in Whitton Dean that.

THEO: The houses are a bit big for us to be honest. No kids.

REG: Think of the money you've saved. I haven't been skiing for bloody years.

THEO: I saw you vomit earlier. In the copse. I was having a pee.

REG: Food after a bit of a work out, upsets the plumbing.

THEO: But not bananas?

REG: No. I used to be fifteen stone. I play squash three times a week. Never felt better. Apart from the odd chunder.

REG rejoins the huddle. SEAN is writing out the batting order.

WILL: (*To SEAN.*) I'll bat eleven Sean. Knees.

SEAN: No. Ten.

CLIVE: You've been told.

SEAN: Alan's disappeared.

WILL: You mean – gone home?

SEAN: Yeah. Paul – pad up. Me and you can open.

THIZ: Thiz three.

SEAN: Nick, three. Pad up.

THIZ: Thiz four.

SEAN: Clive, four.

THIZ: Thiz five.

SEAN: Olly five.

THIZ: Thiz six.

SEAN: Reg!? Do you bat?

REG: Give it a go.

WILL: You'll have to.

NICK: Who do you bat like man? Geoff Boycott? Viv Richards?

THIZ: Amy Winehouse.

REG: Boycott. Slow but sure. I completed my first hundred when I was fifteen.

CLIVE: How old were you when you started it?

They laugh.

REG: Fifteen.

THIZ: Thiz seven.

SEAN: Thiz, seven.

THIZ: Yes!!!!

SEAN: Theo, eight; Rubes, nine; Will ten.

Those who need to pad up, pad up.

THEO: I'll umpire the first ten Sean.

THEO heads over to the tea table.

SEAN: Ta. Er… Thiz, can you umpire for me? Ten overs.

PAUL: I'm not batting if Thiz is umpiring.

WILL: I'll do it.

SEAN: Ta. I'm gonna have a word with Bernard.

SEAN heads for stage right passing the tea table as he goes.

THEO: Sean!

SEAN: Yeah?

THEO: Relax.

SEAN: Yeah. Have you got a tea there?

THEO pours.

THEO: How's Cath?

SEAN: I can't afford to move out. But I can't afford not to.

THEO: It's that bad is it?

SEAN: I go to bed every night thinking about killing myself.

THEO: You wouldn't kill yourself.

SEAN: I'm the type apparently. Like farmers.

THEO: You're a journalist. Vets – they're top of the league. They know how to do it and they've got the tools to do it right there in the drawer.

SEAN: I just want my life back Theo. I spend the whole of my life doing things I don't want to do.

THEO: It's become very difficult for your generation. You marry too late.

SEAN: She hasn't spoken to me today, because I'm coming here. It is a deliberate attempt by her to destroy the only source of joy left in my life. You know, I mean, apart from the kids.

WILL: Has she told you to give up cricket?

SEAN: I can't give it up. It's who I am.

THEO: It's a long day, a cricket match. Seven, eight hours.

SEAN: I did all the shopping yesterday and took them both to the Natural History museum. I sanded down one of her fucking pine doors. Every Saturday is me working to buy a pass for myself for Sunday.

THEO: That's how marriages work.

SEAN walks off.

THIZ: (*To WILL.*) What's your Ellen doing now?

WILL: It's Beth you fancy.

THIZ: Who said anything about fancying anyone?

WILL: Ellen is 'reading' media studies at Loughborough. Beth is at Sheffield Hallam – Applied Modern Languages. And Daniel, not that you're interested in him, is doing an MBA in Newcastle – I think. None of them have been taught how to think, and consequently all three of them are morally illiterate. The only thing any of them will be able to do is get a job.

NICK: They're students. Sex and drugs and rock and roll.

WILL: I hope they are doing sex and drugs and rock and roll. It's the way my children seem to accept, unquestioningly, that all Israelis are Nazis; America is evil, obviously; Hamas are –

CLIVE: – should I be taking notes or is there a hand out at the end?

WILL: I don't mind if they do crack, get pregnant, drop out, but to end up terminally credulous – breaks my heart.

CLIVE: I posit this, your children take these positions because of who you are, what you once were, and what you now say publicly?

WILL: Perhaps.

RUBEN: I'm not stupid.

CLIVE: No Rubes! You are Hope!

THIZ: (*To WILL.*) Have you finished?

WILL: Yes. Sorry.

THIZ: Good. I'm gonna get on with this sandwich now, alright?

Some giggles. silence

NICK: Fifty today boys. Fifty.

PAUL: I don't actually see what a coach could teach me.

CLIVE: Grace.

PAUL: You what?

CLIVE: Fucking grace!

CLIVE gets up and goes over to the tea table. OLLY sees this and follows. WILL goes to LEN.

WILL: We're batting now, Dad.

LEN: William?

WILL: Yes, it's me.

LEN: I don't like Paul. He'll kill this club.

WILL: Yes, I know he will. Do you need anything?

LEN: (*Barely audible.*) Son. Can you tell your mother all about it.

WILL: She knows 'all about it'.

LEN: Who told her?

WILL: You did. Yesterday.

LEN: How did she tek it?

WILL: Very badly. She's not talking to you.

LEN: You'd better not tell her then. I'd like a ciggie. Olly's got some Marlborough Lites.

Over at the tea table, OLLY and CLIVE. CLIVE is reading PAUL's speech.

OLLY: I'm glad you can make the wedding.

CLIVE: I wouldn't miss it for the world.

OLLY: Her parents are…they're really bloody difficult, her dad was in the Army for twenty-five years you know. I wondered, if you could do the speech, the best man speech? I was gonna ask Paul to be best man, but can you imagine what kind of a speech he would make?

CLIVE: Yes I can.

OLLY: You wouldn't have to do any planning or anything it's just the speech.

CLIVE: Olly, I would consider it an honour, but –

OLLY: – and if you could look at my speech for me, please, just have a read, tell me what you think, I'd appreciate that.

OLLY gives him his speech which is two pages of A4 stapled together.

CLIVE: It would be a pleasure. I'd love to. Does Paul know he's not going to be best man?

OLLY: I'd better tell him eh?

CLIVE: Ya. He'll presume.

OLLY: Right.

REG gets his Blackberry out of his bag and fiddles with it.

THIZ: What's that?

REG: It's a Blackberry. Couldn't live without it matey. Wupse! Fuck! Pressed the wrong tit.

THIZ: I'm gonna get one of them. Do they do really big ones?

REG: Smaller the better innit.

THIZ: Since when?

WILL goes over to OLLY.

WILL: Olly!? Len really wants a cigarette.

OLLY: That's alright.

OLLY stands and goes over to LEN.

LEN: Ta son. Light it for us will yer.

OLLY takes the cigarette and lights it for LEN. He gives it to him.

Getting married eh, Olly?

OLLY: Yeah.

LEN: You know you're making a terrible mistake don't you.

OLLY: Yeah.

LEN: We had a lad from Saint Lucia in the team…must've been the seventies. Rennie Greaves. Nice lad. Do you know him?

OLLY: (*He's answered this many times before.*) No, I don't know him Len.

Silence.

LEN: Ta.

OLLY: If you want another one. Just give me a shout. Alright?

OLLY returns to the huddle.

WILL: Thanks.

REG: Where are you from then Olly?

OLLY: Crouch End.

REG: I mean originally.

OLLY: Bury St Edmunds.

REG: Constable country.

OLLY: Yeah.

REG: Yeah, he wouldn't get his brushes out for this would he?

OLLY: I like the city. I don't like the country. If you're black, they look at you funny.

REG: What's your line of work then?

OLLY: I work for the British Council.

REG: Right. What's that, kinda race relations?

OLLY: No. It's cultural imperialism. I'm taking the Tate Modern's Death and Sex Exhibition out to Uzbekistan next month.

REG: Right.

OLLY: Did you see it?

REG: Death and Sex? No, I must've missed that one.

Enter SEAN.

SEAN: Alright! Team talk! Come on!

CLIVE: We never have team talks.

SEAN: Today's different. Nick! Paul! Come on!

They form a half circle around SEAN.

I've spoken to Bernard. I told him I was unhappy with their umpiring, specifically the decisions on the LBWs. I said I thought his umpires were protecting his openers on account of the fact that they are neck and neck in the averages. Absolutely incredible…

CLIVE: – he admitted it?

SEAN: Yeah. He said he'd be happy if we play the rest of the game without LBs.

THIZ: Great!

SEAN: No! It is not great! It's the polar opposite of great. It's shit. The essence of any game is its rules. This is not tiddlewinks. Our umpires, we, are gonna apply the laws to the letter. Anyone out there umpiring, if anyone is out LBW you give them. And if you're batting and get an edge to the keeper – you walk before the umpire has a chance to give you out. We're gonna play this game how it's supposed to be bloody played. OK. Hundred and eighty is not an easy score in thirty-five overs, but we've done it before. Remember Osterley last year. The first target I want anyone to worry about is the first hundred. If we get that in twenty-five overs we're alright. They've tried to cheat us out of this game, they've admitted it, so whatever happens we've won already, morally. But that's not enough for me, and it shouldn't be enough for you. I want to teach them a lesson, so they'll think twice before they try this again. Go out there, concentrate, and we'll beat these fucking cheats.

SEAN breaks away from the group. The others stand, somewhat stunned.

OLLY: Yo!

NICK: Woo!

THIZ: Kaw! Look! I've got a hard on!

To black. Interval.

Act Three

Ten minutes later. The cuckoo again. RUBEN looks after the old scoreboard. The total needed score is set at the bottom and reads 181. WILL is knelt down, near the tea things, tying his shoe laces. THEO is stage right clearing up tea things. SEAN and PAUL are getting ready to bat, ie, strapping on pads etc. Birdsong and almost idyllic.

WILL: (*To THEO.*) I'm getting old. When I was tying my shoe laces just then, I said to myself, 'Is there anything else I can do whilst I'm down here'.

THEO: I can hear a cuckoo! Bird song in the city – beautiful! Can you hear it?

They all listen hard. There is birdsong but no cuckoo. The electronic beep of REG's Blackberry.

REG: (*On the Blackberry.*) Train crash in the Philippines. Two hundred dead.

Enter BERNARD carrying some used paper plates. He puts these down on the table.

BERNARD: I worked out what the problem is with your new scoreboard. All objects have an inherent spectroscopy. White, specifically gloss white, reflects the sun, creating glare.

BERNARD leaves.

THEO: Deborah has been offered a sabbatical from work. She's suggesting we live in the Perigord for six months, a kind of trial, to see if we could live there permanently, and to discover what we miss.

WILL: Six months, across the cricket season?

THEO: You guessed. How's Harriet?

WILL: We haven't made love since 9/11.

THEO: I heard you on 'The Moral Maze' last week. I really think you should be careful Will.

THEO has six beautiful beach stones in his hand.

WILL: What beautiful stones.

THEO: Yes. The Sunday of the Beamers match, I was on Eastbourne beach with Deborah. I'd wanted to play, couldn't, and so did the next best thing – scoured the beach for umpiring stones.

WILL: I've wasted the whole of my life playing this game. It's claimed my knees, and it fills every spare synapse in my brain. Not even sure I like it anymore.

WILL goes over to LEN.

SEAN: (*To PAUL.*) Are you ready?

PAUL is in a world of his own, and doesn't hear.

CLIVE: Communication. The key to an effective opening partnership.

PAUL: What?

WILL: Alright Dad? I'm umpiring, for the first ten.

LEN: (*Very weak.*) I think I'm going.

WILL: Well, no-one's stopping you.

LEN: The best moments of my life have happened on this pitch.

WILL: I won't tell my mother you said that.

THEO joins WILL.

THEO: Ready? You and Harriet must come round for dinner sometime –

WILL and THEO walk off to the centre. PAUL has picked up OLLY's bat.

NICK: Go on lads!

OLLY: (*To PAUL*) Are you going to borrow my bat?

PAUL: Yeah. My bat's split. I told you.

PAUL sets off on his own to the middle.

SEAN: Paul! I'd like us to walk out together, like members of the same team.

PAUL tuts and waits.

SEAN: Call OK. Shout loud. 'WAIT' or 'YES'. No 'NOs'. OK?

PAUL: What's wrong with 'NO'?

SEAN: It sounds like 'GO'.

PAUL: No it doesn't. Go's got a Gu in it.

SEAN: Oh piss off.

PAUL turns and heads off.

NICK: Play your natural game Sean!

WILL: (*Off.*) No bails! Bernard!? Have you got our bails?

BERNARD: (*Off.*) They should be in the umpires' coats.

WILL: (*Off.*) Yes, but whose umpires' coat?

BERNARD: (*Off.*) Whose coats are those? They look like ours.

WILL: (*Off.*) These coats are ours Bernard.

The huddle is now giggling somewhat.

CLIVE: Bernard. He's the human equivalent of spam email isn't he?

NICK: Somebody somewhere loves him I bet.

THIZ: She's over there, lime green shorts.

CLIVE: Forget nature's beauty, birdsong, flowers – the fact that even Bernard has found love is the best argument there is for the existence of God.

NICK laughs. THIZ sits up. Enter WILL. He goes to the kit bag.

WILL: They've lost our bloody new bails.

NICK: Hurry up Skip, rain's forecast.

WILL picks up a pair of old bails and runs back out to the middle.

OLLY: (*Reading from the Sundays.*) What did Reg Varney do on June twenty-seventh nineteen sixty-seven that no-one had ever done before?

THIZ: He fucked a polar bear.

Some laughter.

OLLY: He was the first man to use a hole in the wall cash machine.

REG: First ATM! Course. Obvious!

CLIVE: Reg Varney might have been the first 'celebrated individual' to use an ATM, but they would have been testing that ATM in a live situation for a whole month before they let him anywhere near it. The only certain truth here is that Reg Varney was *not* the first person to use an ATM.

NICK: You're questioning the nature of truth again.

CLIVE: That's why we're here isn't it?

THIZ: Is that what we're here for?

CLIVE: Why do you think you're on this earth Thiz?

THIZ: Play the bass, don't stand in front of the drummer, look gorgeous.

NICK: You're a simple man.

OLLY: A rock and roll artisan.

THIZ: Eh! That's quite good that. Ruben, giss your pencil.

RUBEN, who is doing the book, gives THIZ a pencil from the scorer's tin.

What was it again!?

OLLY: Baby, I'm a simple man -

NICK: – baby, I'm a rock and roll artisan.

REG: That's why we're here. Babies.

CLIVE: Urge, and urge, and urge! Always the procreant urge of the world!

REG: Done my bit mate. I've had four of them. Kaw! Never again.

WILL: (*Off.*) Play!

OPPOSITION: (*Off.*) Bowling Rami!/ Good start!/ Line and length.

OLLY: Quickish.

RUBEN: Bowler's name?

NICK: (*Shouted.*) Bowler's name please!

BERNARD: (*Off.*) Parameswaram!

OLLY mimes not hearing and sticks his hand behind his ear.

(*Off.*)P.A.R.A.M.E.S.W.A.R.A.M.

REG: That's not a name, it's a bloody anagram!

NICK: Steady Paul! Plenty of time!.

OLLY: I caught Paul on the internet last week.

THIZ: Wanking?

OLLY: No. He watched that beheading.

CLIVE: Oh no! That boy is sick.

OLLY: He said he wanted to feel something.

REG: Islam? It's a fucking death cult mate!

CLIVE: I know a way of getting rid of Osama Bin Laden. We'd never hear from him again.

NICK: Yeah? What?

CLIVE: Get my agent to represent him.

OLLY/NICK: (*Laugh.*)

CLIVE: Good shot big fellah!

Applause.

REG: My daughter had a couple of Muslim friends, at primary school, and every year she invited them to her birthday party. Did they come? Never.

NICK: Two there boys! Come on!

REG: I took it up with their dads, in the playground, they both had the same excuse, grandma was ill. Huh! Do I look stupid?

CLIVE: Reg, you'd be offering ham sandwiches, vodka, competitive pass the parcel.

REG: I invited them into my house, and they wouldn't come. How do you explain that to a five year old?

Silence.

NICK: How's the song going man?

THIZ: I'm stuck.

OLLY: Oi! Paul! Watch the edge of that bat!

Some giggle.

NICK: Four off the over Rubes.

OLLY: Good start.

BERNARD: (*Off.*) Bowler's name is Begum! Like Begun but with an M! M for mother.

OLLY: We can spell Begum Bernard.

NICK: Olly, how about getting married in September or October? You know, outside of the cricket season. We're gonna miss a game.

OLLY: She wants an August wedding, in Cornwall, by the sea. Don't ask me why.

CLIVE: Thiz! Have you got any advice to Olly about marriage?

THIZ: If you tour Denmark, don't take her with you.

OLLY: Have you got a girlfriend Thiz?

THIZ: Yeah. Sasha.

CLIVE: And what does she do?

THIZ: Anything. You've only got to ask nicely.

NICK: (*To CLIVE.*) Why don't you and Sian get married?

CLIVE: If it ain't bust don't fix it.

THIZ: Yeah. Must be ten years.

CLIVE: Thirteen.

OLLY: And you love each other?

CLIVE: What the fuck is this? A soap opera? I refuse to talk to you lot about my emotional life –

NICK: Beamer!

Sound of ball on skull. NICK and OLLY jump to their feet.

OLLY: Top edge! He's got it in the eye. Shit!

CLIVE: Where's the first aid box!?

NICK: Oh God!

OLLY: We don't have one.

WILL: (*Off.*) There's a first aid kit in my campervan!

CLIVE: Water.

NICK: Has anyone got water?

WILL: (*To NICK.*) Nick! The keys to the van are in the valuables bag!

NICK picks up the valuables bag. He picks out the keys and exits to the van. CLIVE exits to inspect SEAN. Sound of camper van door opening.

THIZ: What rhymes with artisan?

OLLY: Parmesan.

RUBEN: Anything with 'man' at the end.

THIZ: Fireman. Elephantman. Bedpan. Bedpanman. Not much of a song is it?.

Enter from stage left THEO, CLIVE, and SEAN. CLIVE holding SEAN's bat and gloves. His whites are blood stained from a bad cut over his eye. NICK has the first aid box. BERNARD accompanies.

SEAN: I'm alright. It's alright.

OLLY: That was a beamer.

NICK: Was it deliberate?

THEO: Nick, please! I can't imagine that he meant it. Now, Sean, listen to me, I want you to close your eye, I'm just going to have a look.

THEO inspects the cut. WILL goes to the van and returns with a green first aid box.

NICK: Three stitches there man.

BERNARD: Sutures. Now, I recommend that we wash the conjunctiva with clean water.

THEO: Bernard! I'm a doctor, the very worst thing one can do when there is bleeding from a cut on the supra orbital bridge is to wash the conjunctiva.

BERNARD: Well, that's what I'd do.

BERNARD leaves.

THIZ: Why is it you can never find a sniper when you really need one?

THEO: You'll have to go to A and E.

SEAN: No, I'm not going. Just patch it up Theo.

THEO: No! You're going to need stitches.

THIZ: Sutures.

SEAN: I'm not going! Alright. Just patch me up. Nick, stick a laggy plast on here will you.

NICK: With that, you godda go hospital man.

SEAN: I can still see.

THEO: Sean, I'm telling you to go to –

SEAN: – I'm not going Theo! I've just got me eye in out there.

THEO storms off in a huff.

Nick, patch me up. Hurry up!

NICK and CLIVE patch up the cut.

THIZ: We had a teacher my school just like Bernard. They said he was a paedophile.

OLLY: Did he abuse you?

THIZ: Never touched me. But, what he did do, he used to pay me ten bob to wank him off.

They laugh.

SEAN: Will you shut up Thiz, you're making me laugh.

OLLY: That's child abuse! Him getting you to wank him off, that is him abusing you.

REG is miming that OLLY and THIZ should care about RUBEN listening.

THIZ: He never touched me! And, it was my idea in the first place. I needed the money. I said to him, if you give me ten bob, I'll wank you off. They say all the best ideas are simple, don't they.

CLIVE: There you go big fellah!

NICK: Come on Sean man! Give 'em hell!

SEAN heads back out. He heads straight out.

NICK: Steps!

OLLY: Pavilion!

SEAN changes direction without comment and exits stage right, and down the steps.

THIZ: (*Writing.*) Lollipopman!

NICK: What would you have done if you hadn't become a rock and roll legend?

THIZ: Dunno. Job where you don't have to do much; girls; drugs; loads of money; no lifting. I wouldn't mind being information officer at Stonehenge, cos they don't know anything about it, so if anyone asks anything you just say 'Dunno'.

NICK: Excuse me sir, who built this stone circle?

THIZ: Dunno.

OLLY: When was it built?

THIZ: Dunno.

CLIVE: *S'il vous plaît, Monsieur, est-ce que ce monument megalithique circulaire représente un temple au soleil?*

THIZ: (*Beat.*) Dunno. Get off the fucking grass! Next!

THIZ/NICK/OLLY/CLIVE laugh

OLLY: Oh Paul! You dickhead!

Owzats etc. Cheers off.

CLIVE: That was possibly the ugliest shot I have ever seen.

OLLY: Come on Nick! Fifty today!

CLIVE: Coaching!

PAUL walks off the pitch, and NICK walks on. They cross. RUBEN is writing in the book and then puts up 42 for 2 on the scoreboard.

PAUL: I think there's something wrong with the pick up on your bat Olly.

CLIVE: Oh dear Olly, Paul was out because there's something wrong with the pick up on your bat.

PAUL: Gimme a cigarette.

OLLY chucks his cigarettes over. PAUL lights one.

OLLY: What's the pick up like on that ciggie?

PAUL: Alright. I find the first three minutes after you're out, really existentially threatening. It's a Joy Division, Ian Curtis interlude. When I got that duck against East Sheen, I came within a whisker of self harming.

OLLY: Bowled him!

Laughter off.

CLIVE: Oh no! Who?

Cheering off. Mixed with impolite laughter.

OLLY: Sean.

RUBEN: Bowled Begum.

REG: They're a mouthy bunch aren't they.

OLLY: They're laughing at us. They think we're useless.

CLIVE: It's a situation peculiar to this level of cricket. An ordinary team get a big score and then, fielding second, pick up two quick wickets. They are then inexorably sucked into the delusion that they might be, after all, gods. What is required now is a hero – late thirties, handsome, and ostentatiously well educated. Said hero goes out there tonks two fours in quick succession and it all goes fucking quiet!

OLLY: – yo!

CLIVE: It's not the two fours that shut them up, it's the collective smack of epiphany. The realisation that they're not gods after all, but overweight, middle-aged men stuck in loveless marriages. Goodbye gentlemen! I may be some time!

CLIVE strides out to the middle with utter confidence.

REG: Go on Clive matey!

THIZ: I love him.

OLLY: Brilliant man!

RUBEN: Good luck Clive.

REG: I wish I'd learnt to talk. At my school they just wanted you to shut up.

Enter SEAN. RUBEN changes the scoreboard to read 2 wickets down for 11 runs.

OLLY: Bad luck Sean.

SEAN: Sorry boys.

THIZ: Shoulda swiped it out the ground mate. That's what I'm gonna do. With my new bat. Two hundred and forty quid. Oh yes.

OLLY: Shot Nick!

RUBEN: I love that shot of Nick's.

OLLY: I did a cover drive for four last year.

RUBEN: I remember. Wandsworth Cowboys.

THIZ How many did you get that day?

OLLY: Four.

They laugh.

Christmas Eve. First time I'd met her parents, and she hadn't told them.

THIZ: What?! She hadn't told them you can't bat!

SEAN: (*Laughs.*) Mad Christmas present. A black son in law. Sorry.

OLLY: I couldn't sleep. I was staring at the ceiling getting really angry. But I forced myself to think about that shot against the Cowboys, next thing I knew it was Christmas morning.

SEAN: Shot Clive!

OLLY: There's one of them.

SEAN paces, and looks over RUBEN's shoulder at the book.

SEAN: Twenty-three for two off five.

RUBEN changes the scoreboard. SEAN goes over to the tea things and mixes himself an orange squash.

PAUL: If we lose this game, which looks likely, I'd blame Sean's field placing.

OLLY: Nick's not here. Why don't you slag him off while you can?

SEAN: Shot!

OLLY: Shot Clive!

THIZ stands, a rare event in itself, and shouts out to the pitch.

THIZ: Oi Bernard! Go and look for the ball! Ha, ha, ha!

REG: Get a ton off the first twennie, then go nuts with the bat.

OLLY: Piece of piss.

SEAN: 'cept we're playing with ten men, and we've already lost two wickets.

OLLY: We're gonna need Alan.

RUBEN adjusts the scoreboard. SEAN finds his phone in the valuables bag, dials a number and goes walkabout.

Can you throw a couple of balls at me Ruben please?

RUBEN: I'm doing the book.

OLLY: Paul. Do the book can you? I want to try and get my eye in.

RUBEN: This is Paramaswaram.

PAUL takes the book. SEAN is on the phone to ALAN. OLLY and RUBEN go upstage and RUBEN bowls at OLLY and OLLY pats it back and in between patting it back mimes some extraordinary shots which Viv Richards might eschew.

REG: Nice bunch of lads.

PAUL: Most of them are resistant to change.

REG: Yeah?

PAUL: I'd like to play more games in North London. But they've always played here.

REG: It's a bit skuzzy here innit.

PAUL: Here is the official epicentre of skuzz.

SEAN: Shot Clive! Run 'em up. Three there! One for the throw, come on!

PAUL: I'm gonna go for the captaincy at the AGM. That's a no ball. You see, no signal. I can't put it in the book. Over shoulder height. If we lose by one run. You see no-one in this club knows how to umpire – properly. I'm taking a course at the moment.

REG: I hate umpiring.

PAUL: That's because you don't know the rules.

REG: It's not that, I know the rules.

PAUL: If you're playing a shot and the ball hits your pad outside the line of off stump, and the ball looks like it would hit middle stump. Is that out?

REG: Isn't it?

PAUL: No.

REG: Why not?

PAUL: The rules innit. (*Beat.*) Pitches outside leg?

REG: Not out. I know that.

SEAN: (*On the phone.*) – Alan it reflects the sun… Look, I want you back here to bat, to win this match for me…yeah.

(*To WILL/THEO indicating change of umpires.*) Will! Theo! Umpires! Paul, can you umpire for me please. Ten overs Reg? How do you feel about umpiring?

REG: I'm a bit rusty on the rules skip.

SEAN: Alright, I'll go. Shot Nick!

OLLY: What's he on now?

PAUL: Twennie odd…

PAUL pulls himself to his feet. WILL and THEO enter from the centre. They are both holding umpire's coats. They help SEAN and PAUL on with the coats and pass over their six stones. WILL goes straight over to his dad.

SEAN: Rubes! Can you get back on the book please.

RUBEN: Alright.

THEO: Nick is batting beautifully.

OLLY: He might get his fifty.

WILL checks LEN, who is asleep.

REG: Shot Clive!

OLLY: Backing up! Come on! There's a three there!

REG: Seventy-four off thirteen.

RUBEN: Dad? Can we have a take away tonight? Curry.

WILL: Depends on whether your mother gets arrested. If she does – then yes.

THEO: Does Harriet get arrested often?

WILL: Three times this year already. She loves it.

BERNARD: (*Off.*) Change of bowler. Colman!

WILL: 'Like the mustard'.

BERNARD: (*Off.*) LIKE THE MUSTARD! C –

THIZ: What's he think we are?

BERNARD: – O –

THIZ: – stupid?

BERNARD: – L –

THIZ: (*Shouted.*) We can spell Mustard!

WILL: Colman.

RUBEN: How do you spell Colman…like the mustard?

They laugh.

SEAN: (*Off.*) C.O.L.E.M.A.N.

THEO: No. There's no E in the mustard Colman.

BERNARD: (*Off.*) Can you keep the overs up to date please!

THIZ: Oh yeah, like you did for us?

WILL comes over. RUBEN puts down the book.

WILL: I'll do it.

RUBEN: Fourteen overs gone! Seventy-seven!

WILL changes the scoreboard.

THEO: Six! Oh dear! There's a man on the boundary.

Cheers off.

WILL: Who's out?

RUBEN: Clive. Caught Pilger, bowled Begum.

THEO: Good luck Olly. Concentrate!

THIZ: Yeah, don't think about sex! Ha, ha!

OLLY walks out to the middle. CLIVE comes in and walks straight into the copse having thrown his bat down violently into his bag.

CLIVE: (*Off, in the copse.*) Shit! Fuck! You stupid bastard!

WILL: Pad up Reg.

REG: Righteo!

REG goes into the copse.

WILL: Where's he going? Thiz. Get your pads on.

THIZ: Me? What for?

WILL: 'cos I'm telling you.

THIZ: Alright dad.

CLIVE re-appears.

CLIVE: Sorry team. I failed you.

During the next THIZ puts his pads on. As he is doing this REG is heard to be vomiting in the copse. THEO is aware of this.

WILL: What's going on?

THEO: Reg. He's not well.

WILL: I could have told you that.

THEO: He's lost two stone this year by 'eating bananas'.

RUBEN having seen THIZ padding up, also begins to pad up.

CLIVE: Beautiful shot Nicky!

WILL: Look out! Heads!

RUBEN: Six!

WILL, RUBEN and CLIVE indicate a six by raising both arms. The ball comes skying towards them and goes over them into the copse. RUBEN starts to go after it.

THEO: Stay there Ruben! I'll go.

THEO goes into the copse. He can see REG throwing up. He comes out with the ball and throws it back into the middle. WILL changes the scoreboard to read 83 for 4 off 16. REG comes out the copse and goes to get a drink from the tea table.

THIZ: Ku Klux Klan.

WILL: Have you joined?

THIZ: Rhymes with artisan.

WILL: (*To THEO.*) I think Reg wants to talk to you. Go on! You're a doctor and a Christian. Get over there and do your stuff.

THEO goes over to the tea table.

THEO: Alright Reg! Drinks at twenty overs. Might as well get them ready now.

THEO starts to organise the drinks for the interval.

REG: Think I might have a bidda sunstroke.

THEO: If you live in Whitton Dean why aren't you with me?

REG: I haven't been to the doctor for twennie years.

THEO: How old are you?

REG: Fifty er, bloody hell, er fifty nine.

THEO: A fifty-nine year old man does not lose two stone in eight months by eating bananas. I would recommend that you have some tests, so tomorrow, register with a GP. But for now, get your pads on – you're in next.

OLLY: (*Off.*) Yes!

NICK: (*Off.*) No! Go back!

RUBEN: This is a run out!

THIZ: It's comedy cricket.

VOICES: (*Off.*) Howzat!/How is that!

CLIVE: He's given it.

WILL: You're in Reg.

REG: Sorry boys! I'm not padded up. Can –

WILL: – Thiz! Get out there.

THIZ: Eh?

WILL: Reg isn't ready yet. You're in now.

THIZ: But I'm not dressed.

THIZ puts his helmet.

WILL: Just get out there you big wuss!

THIZ wanders towards the wicket without a bat, then turns and comes back.

THIZ: Forgot my bat. Haven't got my box on. Does anyone want a list of the ways in which I'm not prepared? Put that song in my bag, and don't read it. Giss it here. I don't trust you lot!

CLIVE gives him the song, and he puts it in his pocket. He roots around in his bag for his box. OLLY enters from the field. He throws his bat down, goes for a therapeutic wander around the grass upstage.

WILL: Come on Thiz! Bernard'll time you out, you know he will.

THIZ picks up his bat, finds his box and then puts his helmet on.

THIZ: I'm scared.

THIZ walks out to the wicket, putting his box in as he goes.

WILL: Ruben. Get your grandad to drink some water. He's sick of me.

RUBEN goes to the tea table to get some water and goes to LEN.

RUBEN: Some water here grandad.

LEN: Get a job.

RUBEN: What?

He grabs RUBEN's wrist. RUBEN is alerted, focused.

LEN: A job you like. And a hobby. And a wife. You can't live your life without giving yourself to a woman. You got that?

RUBEN: Job, hobby, wife.

LEN: Aye. Now. I want to tell you, Pegasus Bridge. I was a coward.

RUBEN: But you went. (*Beat.*) You were there.

LEN: I was no fucking use to anyone. That's all, go on. Get back to the lads.

RUBEN: You've got hold of my arm.

LEN: Aye.

LEN lets go his arm. RUBEN goes back to the group.

WILL: I've heard you're very good in this new thing at the Gate.

THEO: Is it in French? Just that I'm working on my French.

CLIVE: It's a translation.

WILL: You've got ten years before you retire to France.

THEO: Yes, but when we do go to live there, permanently, we're determined not to do that ex-pat thing of whist drives, and –

WILL: – Cricket?

THEO: There are cricket teams in the Perigord but I'm determined not to play.

CLIVE: You should play it on their village greens! Under their noses!

WILL: Every immigrant community that comes into this country – we bend over backwards to encourage them to keep their lousy cultures ticking over –

THEO: – lousy cultures? Will!

WILL: Not just ticking over, flourishing, expanding and yet you, with the most beautiful gift on earth –

CLIVE: – cricket.

WILL: – daren't play it in France for fear of offending the locals.

THEO: I didn't say 'daren't'.

WILL: Self-hatred is the cancer at the heart of our nation. If we're not gnawing away at our own back legs in an orgy of self-repudiation, we're not happy.

THEO: Yes, but we want to fit in. To be at least Frenchish.

Blackberry beeps.

REG: (*On his Blackberry.*) Oh bloody hell! One of them London bombers has left hundred and fifty-seven thousand pounds in his will.

WILL: I hope they confiscate that money and build a bloody synagogue.

THEO: Will!?

WILL: They nearly killed me that day. They're racists, they're fascists, and they're bastards.

THEO: Oh come on! If we hadn't got ourselves involved in an illegal war in Iraq –

WILL: – I've got a plan which would make this country completely safe from sexually frustrated Yorkshiremen of a Wahabi Sunni persuasion.

THEO: Oh good heavens!

WILL: It's based on your theory, that we should try not to upset them. So I propose that – one – we should execute all our gay men –

THEO: – oh Will!

WILL: – two – no women can go shopping unless they're wearing a tent.

THEO: – this is silly! –

WILL: – three –replace Politics Philosophy and Economics with chanting the Koran in Arabic.

THEO: – Will, Will, Will!

Some laughter.

What's happened to tolerance?

WILL: You're the one leaving the country.

THEO: I'm upset. I'm very very upset.

WILL: Do you know what upsets me? They look at you, you Theo, possibly the kindest, most soulful individual I have ever met in my entire life and their book tells them that you're nothing, you're going to hell, you're a kaffur.

THEO stands and walks off stage left.

RUBEN: You don't win those arguments with mom.

WILL: Shutup.

Laughter. LEN dies. Nothing noticeable, but this is the moment he stops breathing. Big appeal of Owzat! from off.

OLLY: Oh no!

CLIVE: Sean's given it.

WILL: Who's out?

CLIVE: Nick.

WILL: Shit. What was he on?

RUBEN: Forty-eight.

CLIVE: Nick's not happy.

WILL: You're in Reg.

REG: Any instructions?

CLIVE: Yes! Could you score a quick, stylish century please!

REG: Do me best.

REG exits stage right and on to the field via the steps. NICK comes back off the pitch to a big round of applause and 'well batted' from the opposition.

WILL: Well batted Niranjan!

CLIVE: Bad luck Nick! Brilliant.

OLLY: Great stuff Nick.

NICK: That wasn't out man. It pitched outside off, I was playing a shot, not out. That was Sean doing his bloody moral…whatever… thing.

CLIVE: Sorry, explain.

NICK: What Sean said about LBWs at tea man. He's given me out man, cos he has to give someone out LBW, to show that he's a man of his word.

(*Beat.*) How many did I get?

RUBEN: Forty-eight.

NICK: Shit! Forty-eight?

CLIVE: Pad up Rubes!

RUBEN: I'm not next. It's Theo.

CLIVE: Exactly. Give me the book.

RUBEN hands the book over to CLIVE, and RUBEN gets padded up.

WILL: Get Sean back here. We're losing more wickets on the boundary than we are out there on the pitch.

CLIVE: (*Standing and walking forward.*) Sean! Sean! Change of umpires!

WILL: Who's going out?

OLLY: I'll go.

WILL: Bloody hell! Heads!

CLIVE: Watch out!

WILL: Reg! Shot Reg!

RUBEN retrieves the ball from the copse. Enter SEAN.

SEAN: What's occurring?

WILL: Theo's gone off in a huff.

SEAN: Eh?

CLIVE: Will suggested that this country's pusillanimous liberal left political elite have established the orthodoxy of multiculturalism to such an extent that the nation is sleepwalking towards the establishment of a European Islamic caliphate.

SEAN: Who's in next?

WILL: Theo!

CLIVE: Ruben's padded up.

SEAN: So we're down to nine men. Brilliant.

Enter ALAN. He is acknowledged by SEAN. No-one else says anything.

WILL: Heads!

SEAN: Shot Reg!

NICK retrieves the ball and throws it back. RUBEN indicates six runs.

CLIVE: Hundred up.

All on the boundary clap.

NICK: Well done lads!

SEAN: Keep it up Thiz!

WILL: Thiz is playing well.

Laughter off.

What's he done?

CLIVE: He's coming off. He's not out, what is it?

Enter THIZ with broken bat, in two parts.

THIZ: Two hundred and forty quid. I'll get a Toyota next time.

WILL: You hadn't knocked it in. I told you!

SEAN: You're doing well Thiz, keep your head down, listen to Reg.

THIZ: I'm not listening to him. He's a nutter.

SEAN: Running, I'm talking about.

THIZ walks out.

(*To ALAN.*) Come over here.

SEAN drags ALAN over to the tea table.

Are you gonna bat for me?

ALAN: I only came back for my watch.

SEAN: No! You're batting. The only way I'll exclude you from batting today is if you supply me with a death certificate.

ALAN: I don't know why you get so excited, it's a Sunday game, a friendly.

SEAN: Saturday, Sunday, Monday! What are you telling me? That's there's a time when you don't have to do the right thing?

ALAN: Who? Me?

SEAN: You don't need to prove your worth to us by building scoreboards. Thiz is not a great cricketer, and he's not in the team 'cos he's famous or 'cos he tells jokes, he's in the team 'cos he rings up and says he's available. You're in the team, you're wanted. It might not be love mate, but it's as near as we're gonna get alright?! So, are you gonna bat for me or not?

ALAN: I'm not batting at eleven.

SEAN: I'll sort that. I'm gonna go get a cigarette.

ALAN: Here.

ALAN produces a packet of 20. SEAN takes one.

Don't tell anyone.

ALAN lights SEAN's cigarette for him.

How old are your kids now?

SEAN: Three and five.

ALAN: And you're still together?

SEAN: Just.

ALAN: Difficult yeah?

SEAN: My life's fucked mate.

ALAN: At the end of the day, when all's said and done, if you've godda go you've godda go. I've been divorced twice.

SEAN: I didn't know you'd been married twice.

ALAN: Been married three times. I've got five kids. My eldest, he's sixteen.

SEAN: Does he play?

ALAN: I don't know.

SEAN: We need a bit of new blood.

ALAN: I'll ask.

SEAN: Go and get your pads on.

ALAN goes over to the group. SEAN follows a couple of moments later.

NICK: Shot Thiz! (*Beat.*) So where did that ball pitch Sean?

SEAN: What ball?

NICK: You know man, you know what you did.

SEAN: What are you on about?

NICK: I wasn't out.

WILL: Come on lads! Forget it.

NICK: Sean said at tea, didn't you man, you said they offered no LBWs for our innings and yeah, –

SEAN: – the rules –

NICK: – listen to me yeah – you made this big deal out of playing the rules properly, well what I'm saying is that you gave me out cos -

SEAN: – you were out.

NICK: It pitched outside the line, I was playing a shot!

SEAN: It doesn't matter where it pitches on the off side, it's where your leg is that matters.

NICK: Alright, well, my leg was outside the line –

SEAN: – make your mind up. Was the ball outside the line or your leg?

NICK: My leg!? And that's not out unless the umpire's actually itching –

SEAN: – itching?

NICK: – yeah itching to give someone out LBW – because of –

SEAN: – because he wants his team to lose?

NICK: – cos of what he said.

SEAN: You were plumb Nick.

WILL: Come on lads. We're a team.

NICK: I was on forty-eight.

SEAN: You were on forty-eight when you got hit on the pads in front of the wicket.

NICK: I know you Sean. There are two things, yeah, you enjoy most in this beautiful brilliant game. One is scoring a century and winning the match, and the other is walking, when you've nicked one to the keeper, and only you and the keeper know, you walk, yeah, you get a lot of pleasure from that, yeah. You love walking. You love showing everyone that you play the game properly, fairly, it's like sex for you.

SEAN: Ooooh!

WILL: Eh, come on boys. Forget it.

SEAN: I walk, yes. And I hope that if you're on forty-nine and you nick it to the keeper and no-one hears it, I hope that you walk. Cos I for one don't want to know you if you don't walk.

NICK: (*Quietly.*) I wasn't out was I?

(*Beat.*) You gave me out to prove a point about playing the game fairly when in fact, all you're doing man, is putting yourself at the middle of everything.

(*Beat.*) It's just selfish actually.

(*Beat.*) Was I out?

(*Beat.*) Answer me. You know I wasn't out.

(*Beat.*) I want an answer, man. I know I'm right. Was I out?

SEAN starts sobbing. No-one moves. No-one says anything.

CLIVE: Come on, come on, big fellah. It's alright Sean. You're alright.

SEAN: I can't stand it… I can't stand it…

WILL stands. RUBEN is amazed and stares at SEAN.

WILL: Ruben, come on, I'll throw a few balls at you. Nick can you do the book.

NICK: Yeah, man, giss it here.

WILL and RUBEN go upstage to practice, handing the book over to NICK.

NICK: (*Struggling with the book.*) Who's this bowling Rubes?

RUBEN: Thomas. Pilger is the spin bowler from the other end.

NICK: Got it. Ta, man.

CLIVE: Have we got some water?

NICK: Here.

NICK goes in his own bag and brings out a bottle of water and hands it over.

SEAN: Sorry.

NICK: I'm sorry, actually. Yeah?

SEAN: Alright.

NICK: Cool.

SEAN swigs the water – still sobbing.

BERNARD: (*Off.*) Can you keep the overs up to date please!?

CLIVE: What's the score?

NICK: Hundred and twennie one. Eleven overs left.

BERNARD: (*Off.*) Telegraph!

CLIVE: (*In clear, loud actor's voice.*) The score is One hundred and twenty-one for five off twenty-four overs! And you're holding up play Bernard. They're waiting for you.

NICK: Reg is batting like a train man!

(*Off.*) Howzat!

NICK: What's Thiz doing?

CLIVE: Hit wicket.

NICK: Rubes! You're in.

WILL and RUBEN come down and rejoin the huddle. RUBEN walks out, with a quick look to LEN – who of course is dead.

CLIVE: Concentrate Ruben! Backing up! Think! Cricket brain!

THIZ walks off, not too bothered.

NICK: Batted Thiz. Good stuff man.

THIZ: Hit me own wicket. That bat's a bit longer than I thought.

WILL: Sean, do you want me to pad up or are you going to let Alan go number nine?

SEAN: Er...yeah. Alan nine, Will, ten. Yeah. Sorry.

WILL: No, it's alright. The knees.

THIZ sits back in WILL's chair.

NICK: Full toss. They're bowling bloody beamers at a twelve year old.

WILL: Thirteen.

CLIVE: He's got a helmet on.

ALAN scratches a bit of bare leg.

ALAN: I got really badly bitten last week.

THIZ: What was her name?

ALAN: Midges.

THIZ: Never heard of her.

NICK: Another beamer!

CLIVE: (*Stands.*) Excuse me! We've paid for this pitch, do you mind using it!

They laugh.

NICK: Reg is on forty already.

THIZ: I don't like him.

WILL: I don't like him.

NICK: Alan?

ALAN: What?

NICK: Do you like Reg?

ALAN: No.

CLIVE: He's brilliant. I love him!

NICK: That's cos you're an actor, man, you can see it's a part you could play.

CLIVE: Most actors would play Reg ironically, and that would be a disgrace. I'd do it with beauty, commitment, emphasise the heroic. I would deliver a celebration of England.

SEAN: Lovely shot Ruben!

THIZ: Bloody hell, Sean! Are you here?

SEAN: Yeah.

THIZ: Bit quiet. You're usually biting someone's head off. What's going on?

NICK: Five off the over. Going well.

WILL goes over to LEN with a glass of water. He is intending to tell LEN that RUBEN's batting and give him some water. WILL realises LEN is dead.

WILL: Dad? Jesus. Oh hell, what do I do? Dad!

VARIOUS: Shot Reg! / Heads / Six!

The ball goes flying over the copse into the field beyond. Several of the group on the boundary go after the ball disappearing through the hedge WILL checks LEN's breath and pulse and accepts that he's dead.

SEAN: (*Off.*) Lost ball! Bring a bat someone please!

BERNARD is heard coming off the field via the steps. He appears holding a bat. This he gives to those looking for the ball. He then turns and approaches WILL having looked at the scoreboard.

BERNARD: Will! I think the overs must be wrong. It's twenty-five gone by my calculations. The first over was bowled from the far end, so any over bowled from that end has to be an odd number, but you've got twenty-four on the board. Twenty-four is an even number.

WILL: Fuck off Bernard!

BERNARD stands still but assesses the situation correctlyish and moves off into the copse to help look for the ball.

SEAN: (*Off.*) Found it!

SEAN gives the ball to BERNARD. WILL adjusts LEN's hat and rejoins the others.

NICK: Fifty up Reg!

Applause.

VARIOUS: Keep going Reg! / Come on boys! Another fifty Reg!

WILL: Does anyone have a cigarette?

NICK: Olly.

CLIVE: No they're all gone.

SEAN looks to ALAN. ALAN offers a cigarette to WILL.

NICK: Alan!?

SEAN: Bowled him!

NICK: (*Quietly, ie, not to RUBEN*) Oh bad luck Rubes.

CLIVE: Run those singles Alan!

ALAN walks out. RUBEN comes in to a round of applause from all. He chucks his bat aggressively down, partly from natural frustration but it is also, clearly, learned behaviour.

You'd better get padded up Will.

NICK: Two runs for ten thousand, man. The champagne is on ice.

WILL: There is champagne actually, in the van. In the fridge. If required.

RUBEN: You're smoking.

WILL: No, I'm looking after this for Thiz.

He hands it to THIZ, who takes it.

THIZ: Have you ever tried ciggies Ruben?

RUBEN: Yeah.

THIZ: Waste of money, make you stink, gives you cancer. Don't start, don't be a fool. If you need a high, bit of a rush, you can't beat heroin.

NICK: Lovely shot Reg!

THIZ: It gets a bad press, I know that, but –

WILL: – Thiz!

CLIVE: Good Lord! Reg certainly hits that ball hard.

SEAN: Ten off the over! We could win this you know.

NICK: Three overs left, twenty-two required. Bowler's name please!?

BERNARD: (*Off.*) Mohammad!

ALL: Like the prophet.

BERNARD: (*Off.*) Like the Prophet! M. O. –

NICK: We can spell Mohammad!

THIZ: If you can't spell it just draw a picture.

They laugh.

NICK: Can we just have a day off Islam please!? I'm fucking sick of it man, alright?

CLIVE: There's a single there.

SEAN: Two there! Run 'em up Alan!

WILL: Alan doesn't know what he's doing but he's quick between the wickets.

NICK: Come on Reggie!

CLIVE: Oh. 'Reggie' now is it?

NICK: Yeah, it's Reggie.

THIZ: Big one!

WILL: Heads!

A ball comes sailing over them into the copse. RUBEN goes for the ball and throws it back.

NICK: End of the over. One hundred and seventy for seven. Two overs left.

THIZ: (*Standing.*) Come on boys!

SEAN goes over to the scoreboard and puts the runs up. 170 for 7.

RUBEN: Is grandad alright?

WILL: Yeah.

RUBEN stands as if to go over to LEN. WILL grabs his arm.

He's alright.

RUBEN sits. Enter THEO.

SEAN: You're back.

THEO: How are we doing?

SEAN: Put your pads on. Will's in next, but you know, with his knees.

CLIVE: Bowled him!

SEAN: Who's out?

WILL: Alan.

SEAN: Good! As long as Reg is out there we're alright.

WILL: Sean! Do you want me to go out now, or are we going to wait for Theo?

SEAN: Yeah, yeah, go out now Will. Good luck.

WILL walks out to the wicket passing ALAN as he comes in to applause.

SEAN: Thank you Alan.

WILL: Played Alan.

NICK: Good work man.

ALAN: Inside edge. I should've left it alone.

CLIVE: Bowled by one you should've left alone. The ultimate tragedy.

SEAN changes the wickets on the scoreboard to 8. RUBEN goes over to LEN.

RUBEN: Grandad? Grandad?

NICK: Shot Will!

CLIVE: Three there. Not.

NICK: Go on Will!

They laugh. CLIVE takes rests some paper on his Homer and writes something down.

SEAN: Oh God it's embarrassing.

CLIVE: He should have a runner.

SEAN: That's two runs gone begging there. That's pride. If we lose this game –

CLIVE: – Calm down Sean. He's done the important thing. He's got Reg on strike.

SEAN: What was that, you wrote down?

CLIVE: I took a note of something Reg said earlier. I am now a writer.

SEAN: Why haven't you ever written anything?

CLIVE: Because Reg came into my life for the first time today.

RUBEN: Grandad?

RUBEN walks back to the group. He realises that LEN is dead.

SEAN: We're an ageing team.

CLIVE: What we need is a six foot seven inch sixteen year old fast bowler, with four foot long arms, no brains –

SEAN: – big fast bowler's arse.

THIZ: Big tits.

SEAN: Alan has a teenage son.

ALAN: I'll ask.

NICK: Shot Reggie!

SEAN: (*With arms in the air like a fan.*) Six!

NICK: End of the over. One seven seven. For eight. One over left. And Will is on nine thousand nine hundred and ninety nine runs for the club.

CLIVE: Thank you Bearders.

NICK: He needed eleven at the beginning of the season. Fifteen matches later he needs one.

CLIVE: It's a mini-series.

SEAN: Is that more runs than Len?

RUBEN: Grandad is twelve thousand two hundred and eleven runs.

They all look across to LEN.

CLIVE: Round of applause gentlemen.

They clap.

NICK: Well done Len!

THEO: Is he alright?

RUBEN: He's sleeping.

NICK: Come on Will! One run!

RUBEN: I'll get the champagne.

RUBEN goes to the van.

FARRINGDEN: (*Off.*) How is that! Owzat!

CLIVE: That's not a stumping. His bat's down.

SEAN: Stop begging!

CLIVE: I know Paul, he'll give that, because he wasn't looking.

FARRINGDEN: (*Off.*) Yeah! / Yes! / Woo! / Woo!

SEAN: How can he give that, he didn't see it?

RUBEN arrives with champagne.

CLIVE: Back in the fridge Ruben.

They laugh.

SEAN: Theo. Try and get a single. Get Reggie down that end.

THEO: Yes. Of course. Reggie.

THEO strides out. WILL hobbles back in.

NICK: Bad luck Will!

WILL: Three more games this season.

SEAN changes the scoreboard. Stays beside it now, putting up the score one by one.

SEAN: Five balls left. Five to win.

They're all on their feet and even edge forwards on to the pitch.

NICK: Shot Theo.

THIZ: Two there!

SEAN: No! We want Reg on strike. Stay for one. Oh no! You idiot!

CLIVE: Sean, that's Theo. That's not an idiot.

SEAN puts two more runs up. The board reads 179.

ALAN: What do we need?

CLIVE: Three to win.

SEAN: Four balls left.

VARIOUS: Oooh! OH!

SEAN: Bloody hell, come on. Just get a nick on it.

NICK: Three balls to go.

CLIVE: Come on Theo love.

VARIOUS: Oh! / Fuck. / Groans.

SEAN: We need the ball to hit him on the head and run off for leg byes.

NICK: Two balls to go. Runs required. Three.

SEAN: Get some wood on it!

NICK: Shot Theo!

THIZ: bloody hell!

CLIVE: Four!?

VARIOUS: Yes! / Yo! / Yeah!

They hug, and jump, and cheer, shake hands etc. It clouds over.

CLIVE: What a beautiful shot.

SEAN: Fantastic! Yes!

CLIVE: Well done Sean.

SEAN: Well done guys. Brilliant. Thank you!

VARIOUS: Well done Sean / brilliant Seanie / well skippered. / cheers big fellah.

REG and THEO walk off the field together to applause.

SEAN: Thank you guys. Well batted Reg.

NICK: Brilliant shot man!

SEAN: Guys! Please, clap the fielding team, shake hands.

BERNARD approaches shaking hands with everyone.

Bad luck skip.

The others of Farringden walk off the field and shake hands with everyone, with lots of 'thank yous', 'well bowleds', 'well batteds' etc as appropriate.

WILL: Alan, Ruben, can you get the boundary markers please. Thank you.

WILL starts to pack the bag. REG takes a swig of water. THEO is still having his back slapped. Some individuals get changed back into civvies – these are CLIVE, OLLY, PAUL. The others keep their cricket gear on and pack their civvies into their bags.

REG: What did I get?

NICK: Eighty-four.

THIZ: I got eleven.

REG: Bloody hell! I enjoyed that! That first pint ain't even gonna touch the sides.

CLIVE: I'm available next week. Who's match managing?

WILL: Alan.

ALAN: Anyone else?

SEAN: Yeah.

ALAN: Paul?

PAUL: Yeah.

ALAN: Theo?

THEO: Sorry, not Hampstead Heath. It's a two-hour drive for me.

REG: You can put me down Alan.

SEAN: Er…give Alan your number Reg, and if we don't have eleven from members, you know, people who've paid their annual subs, then we'll give you a ring. Alright?

REG: What's the subs?

SEAN: The amount of the subs is set each year at the annual general meeting.

REG: I'll pay now.

SEAN: Give Alan your number. OK.

REG: OK.

ALAN: I've only got four for next week.

WILL: Ring Gary.

SEAN: Match fees please! Five pounds. Anyone, not going to the pub don't leave without paying.

SEAN goes for his money in his cricket trousers in notes and so separates one five pound note out and puts it in a separate pocket.

THIZ: I haven't got any money.

CLIVE: Impossible. Thiz Carlisle, no money?

THIZ: I had a lot of money in here this morning.

OLLY: We've been done. My cash has gone.

CLIVE: Oh fuck! I had forty pound. Bloody hell!

SEAN: I keep notes in my pocket.

WILL: I did organise a valuables bag. You ignore your elders and betters every week.

THIZ: That little chav, do you remember. It'll be him.

REG: Bastard! Fifty fucking quid! Bastard! I don't believe it. I do not fucking believe it.

NICK: My cash has gone but he didn't take my cards.

THIZ: I got me cards still. Oh alright then, dunt matter, I'll go and get some more.

WILL: Has anyone had cards stolen?

NICK: I'm alright.

CLIVE: No.

OLLY: Just the cash.

ALAN: Got mine.

SEAN: Will, better have a word with Bernard. He might have done them over as well.

WILL: I'll ring the police.

THIZ: Na! It's only cash.

WILL: That's why he didn't take your cards. Hoping we wouldn't phone the police.

THIZ: I'm gonna the pub. I'm not hanging around here waiting for the Old Bill to turn up. I got platinum.

WILL makes the phone call. NICK goes around with a carrier bag picking up litter. Enter BERNARD.

BERNARD: Which pub is it William?

WILL: It's the first one you come to.

BERNARD: Yes, but what is it called?

WILL: The Samuel Beckett.

BERNARD: That's it! I knew it was an Irish playwright who believed in the folly of all human endeavour. Ha, ha!

WILL: We've had cash stolen from our wallets.

BERNARD: Oh dear me.

WILL: Did you see anyone? When we were fielding?

SEAN: Young chavvie-looking white kid, white track suit bottoms.

BERNARD: I was umpiring.

WILL: When I say you, I mean your team, collectively.

BERNARD: I'll ask. Bad luck chaps. Here, we always use a valuables bag.

BERNARD walks off.

SEAN: Ask them why they didn't stop the guy going through our bags. Why they didn't physically challenge him, and restrain him.

NICK: See you in the pub.

WILL: I'm not going to the pub. I'll see you next week Nick.

NICK leaves. WILL is packing the kit bag, tea things etc and doing a reverse of the opening scene, ie, carrying them back to the van. He is given a helping hand by THEO when lifting the kit bag to the van. Having done that they come straight back on.

THIZ: See you Len!

THIZ walks off.

PAUL: Are you staying at the flat tonight?

OLLY: I'm waiting for a text.

PAUL: I've got to show you my speech at some point haven't I.

OLLY: What speech?

PAUL: The best man speech. I'm worried that...well, her parents are snobby aren't they. Are you gonna the pub? I'll talk you through it then.

OLLY: Yeah.

PAUL: Alright.

PAUL walks off.

WILL: Goodbye Paul!

PAUL: What?

WILL: Goodbye.

PAUL: Yeah, see you. What?

WILL collects the old scoreboard and puts it in the van. SEAN leaves.

SEAN: Are you gonna the pub Theo?

THEO: *Bien sûr*! I'll see you in the garden?

SEAN: Yeah.

CLIVE: Sun's gone in.

THEO: Timing. Brilliant.

OLLY: Are you gonna the pub?

CLIVE: Indeed.

OLLY: My lot are a bit arty, you know, but Barbara's...

CLIVE: Let's find five minutes in the pub. OK. See you chaps!

OLLY and CLIVE leave. REG goes over to ALAN who is writing names down for the next week and packing his kit.

REG: I won't need rocking to sleep tonight. Let me give you my number mate.

ALAN offers him the pen and paper he's been using to write next week's team on. REG starts writing down his number.

About the sink. I'll pay you to do it properly.

ALAN: Here's my card.

ALAN gives him a business card.

REG: Ta.

ALAN: I've got a car and a van. The council wouldn't give me planning permission for a double garage. They said it's a policy across the borough. (*Beat.*) It's only a matter of time before you're gonna have to knock that double garage down. See you.

ALAN leaves. THEO and WILL return from the van. THEO has the scorebook.

REG: (*Offering his hand to shake.*) Thanks for the game Will. Been really bloody marvellous.

(*Shaking hands with THEO.*) And –

THEO: Theo.

REG: Theo. Ta pal! I'll get down the doctor's tomorrow.

THEO: I hope you do, but I don't think you will.

REG: No. I will. Something's wrong. I know. Something's...not right. See you in the pub.

REG leaves. WILL and THEO go over to LEN, and wait until everyone else is gone.

WILL: What do I do I have to do now?

THEO: One is supposed to call an ambulance and the police. Paramedics can declare a death. But so can doctors. And I'm a doctor and he's dead. Take him home, put him in his chair, and call his doctor. The only problem is, we don't have a time of death.

WILL: Why would I need to ring the police?

THEO: They get involved if there are any suspicious circumstances. But there aren't. I suspect Len died exactly where he wanted to die.

WILL: Exactly where he wanted to die would be out there on the wicket with a bat in his hand.

THEO: Does Ruben know?

WILL: Ruben!

RUBEN: What?

WILL: Come over here.

RUBEN joins them.

RUBEN: What?

WILL: Grandad's died.

RUBEN: Yeah. I know.

WILL: You know?

RUBEN: I spoke to him, after I was out. He was already dead then.

THEO: How did you know he was dead?

RUBEN: I watched his stomach. It didn't move, you know, with his breathing. He's always asleep at home, and his stomach always moves up and down, not his chest.

THEO: So, time of death, Ruben bowled Pilger six-forty nine.

WILL: So I can move the body, I don't have to ring the police?

THEO: Tell his doctor exactly what happened, give him my number.

WILL: I'm feeling guilty now. But I didn't want the lads to know. There'd be a fuss, and…but now it's beginning to feel, wrong.

THEO: Let's get him in the van.

THEO and WILL pick up LEN and carry him to the van.

WILL: Ruben! Open the sliding door please.

They carry him off. Doors are heard to open and close. They come back for other bits and pieces including RUBEN's bike.

WILL: Are you cycling back?

RUBEN: Yeah.

WILL: Do you mind son? I'd like someone in the van with me.

RUBEN: Alright.

RUBEN puts his bike in the van.

THEO: He was a lovely man. A great man as well. A soldier. My father was a conscientious objector. Will he be buried in Yorkshire?

WILL: No. Cremation.

THEO: And the ashes?

WILL: Where do you think?

THEO looks out to the middle.

THEO: Pegasus Bridge, or out there.

WILL: Out there.

THEO: I'll come in the van with you if you want.

WILL: No, I'll manage. You go to the pub.

WILL and THEO shake hands.

THEO: You must come to stay with us in France.

WILL: France?

THEO: Yes. I'm not going to play again. I was very upset today.

THEO starts to walk off.

(*Off.*) Well batted Rubes!

RUBEN: (*Off.*) Ta.

WILL picks up the deck chair and starts to walk off. He has a glance around and sees an empty cigarette packet which he picks up. He walks off. Sound of camper van door opening. Then Van Morrison kicks in halfway through 'And the Healing has begun'. The engine starts, and the van drives off. There is a distant flash of lightning and then seven seconds later, thunder. Then the rain – an exuberant summer shower, the kind which feels like a celebration.

To black.